75 Baked Potato Recipes

(75 Baked Potato Recipes - Volume 1)

Joy Brannon

Copyright: Published in the United States by Joy Brannon/ © JOY BRANNON

Published on August, 22 2020

All rights reserved. No part of this publication may be reproduced, stored in retrieval system, copied in any form or by any means, electronic, mechanical, photocopying, recording or otherwise transmitted without written permission from the publisher. Please do not participate in or encourage piracy of this material in any way. You must not circulate this book in any format. JOY BRANNON does not control or direct users' actions and is not responsible for the information or content shared, harm and/or actions of the book readers.

In accordance with the U.S. Copyright Act of 1976, the scanning, uploading and electronic sharing of any part of this book without the permission of the publisher constitute unlawful piracy and theft of the author's intellectual property. If you would like to use material from the book (other than just simply for reviewing the book), prior permission must be obtained by contacting the author at author@roastroastroast.com

Thank you for your support of the author's rights.

Content

75 AWESOME BAKED POTATO RECIPES 5

1. Baked Sweet Potato Mash With Crunchy Pecan Sourdough Topping 5
2. Barbecued Spice Rubbed Lamb With Sweet Potato Gratin 5
3. Bean And Potato Bake, 4 Ways Recipe 6
4. Boulangerie Potatoes 6
5. Brie, Thyme And Bacon Dauphinoise Potato 7
6. Celeriac And Sweet Potato Bake 7
7. Cheesy Bean And Potato Bake 8
8. Cheesy Mashed Potato Bake 8
9. Cheesy Potato And Bacon 'lasagne' 9
10. Cheesy Potato Bake 9
11. Cheesy Smashed Baked Potatoes 10
12. Colin's Potato Bake With Pancetta 10
13. Creamy Celeriac And Potato Bake 11
14. Creamy Dairy Free Curried Potato And Pumpkin Bake 11
15. Creamy Kale, Pumpkin And Potato Bake 12
16. Creamy Mashed Potato And Chive Bake .. 13
17. Creamy Potato And Ham Bake With Fresh Rosemary 13
18. Creamy Potato And Kale Gratin 14
19. Creamy Potato And Nutmeg Bake 14
20. Creamy Potato And Rosemary Bake 15
21. Creamy Potato Bacon Bake 15
22. Creamy Potato Bake 16
23. Creamy Scalloped Potato Bake With Pesto And Rocket 16
24. Creamy Scalloped Potato Tray Bake Recipe 16
25. Crispy Garlic And Thyme Boulangere Potatoes 17
26. Crispy Topped Potato Bake 17
27. Double Cheese Sweet Potato Bake Recipe 18
28. Easy Cheese And Tomato Potato Bake 19
29. Easy Creamy Potato Bake 19
30. Extreme Cheese Fondue Potato Pie 20
31. Fennel And Potato Gratin 20
32. Garlic And Rosemary Potato Bake 21
33. Garlic And Rosemary Scalloped Potatoes 21
34. Garlic And Thyme Scalloped Potatoes 21
35. Ham And Leek Potato Gratin Recipe 22
36. Hash Brown Potato Bake Recipe 22
37. Hayden Quinn's Ultimate Sweet Potato Bake Recipe 23
38. Healthier Potato And Sweet Potato Bake . 23
39. Individual Creamy Potato Gratins 24
40. Individual Pumpkin And Gnocchi Bakes . 24
41. Janssons Frestelse (Jansson's Temptation) 25
42. Layered Potato Cake 25
43. Louise's Two Potato Gratin 26
44. Low Fat Creamy Potato Gratin With Parmesan Crumbs 26
45. Mashed Potato And Bacon Bake 27
46. Moroccan Sweet Potato Bake 28
47. Mustard Balsamic Beef With Creamy Potato Bake 28
48. Parmesan, Potato Leek Bake 29
49. Parsnip, Leek And Potato Gratin With Pecan Crumble 29
50. Pommes Anna 30
51. Potato Onion Gratin 30
52. Potato Parsnip Gratin 31
53. Potato And Beef Ragu Lasagne 31
54. Potato And Celeriac Bake 32
55. Potato And Fennel 'bake' Recipe 33
56. Potato And Leek Gratin 33
57. Potato Gratins 34
58. Potato Tortilla 34
59. Potato, Bacon Blue Cheese Bake 35
60. Potato, Bacon And Leek Gratin 35
61. Potato, Blue Cheese And Pine Nut Bake .. 36
62. Prosciutto Stuffed Potato Bake 36
63. Provencal Potato Bake 37
64. Quick Chicken And Garlic Potato 'bake' .. 37
65. Quick Creamy Chicken And Sweet Potato Bake 38
66. Reduced Fat Chicken And Leek Potato Bake 38
67. Scalloped Potatoes 39
68. Simple Potato Bake 39
69. Slow Cooked Sweet Potato Bake 40
70. Swede, Potato And Bacon Gratin 40
71. Sweet Potato And Ricotta Bake 41
72. Sweet Potato Bake 41
73. Sweet Potato Bake With Bacon Crumble .. 42
74. Sweet Potato With Pecan Ginger Crumble

               42
    75. Tartiflette (cheese Potato Bake)................ 43
INDEX **44**
CONCLUSION **46**

75 Awesome Baked Potato Recipes

***

1. Baked Sweet Potato Mash With Crunchy Pecan Sourdough Topping

Serving: 4 | Prep: 15mins | Ready in: 50mins

Ingredients

- 800g orange sweet potato, peeled, coarsely chopped
- 1/3 cup sour cream
- 50g butter
- 100g sourdough bread, cut into 2cm pieces
- 1/2 cup pecans, roughly chopped
- 2 tablespoons maple syrup

Direction

- Preheat oven to 200C/180C fan-forced. Grease a 7cm-deep, 16cm round (4-cup capacity) ovenproof dish.
- Cook sweet potato in a large saucepan of boiling water for 8 to 10 minutes or until just tender. Drain. Return to pan. Add sour cream and 1/2 the butter. Mash until smooth. Season with salt and pepper.
- Combine sourdough and pecans in a small bowl. Place maple syrup and remaining butter in a small heatproof jug. Microwave on HIGH (100%) for 20 seconds or until melted. Spoon mash into prepared dish. Sprinkle with sourdough mixture. Drizzle with maple syrup mixture.
- Bake for 20 to 25 minutes or until bread is golden and crisp. Serve.

Nutrition Information

- Calories: 497.12 calories
- Saturated Fat: 12.7 grams saturated fat
- Total Carbohydrate: 47.9 grams carbohydrates
- Cholesterol: 42 milligrams cholesterol
- Sodium: 305 milligrams sodium
- Total Fat: 29.2 grams fat
- Protein: 7.9 grams protein

2. Barbecued Spice Rubbed Lamb With Sweet Potato Gratin

Serving: 6 | Prep: 10mins | Ready in: 160mins

Ingredients

- 1 tablespoon olive oil
- 2 teaspoons ground coriander
- 1/2 teaspoon dried thyme
- 1 teaspoon garlic powder
- 2.5kg Coles Australian Lamb Whole Leg Roast
- 1 medium leek, thinly sliced
- 1kg gold sweet potato, thinly sliced
- 1 garlic clove, thinly sliced
- 300ml thickened cream
- 1 cup (120g) grated tasty cheddar
- Salad leaves, to serve

Direction

- Preheat a covered barbecue on medium. Alternatively, preheat oven to 200C.
- Combine oil, coriander, thyme and garlic powder in a small bowl. Rub over lamb. Season well. Place lamb in a disposable baking tray. Roast in covered barbecue using indirect heat, or in oven, for 2 hours 30 mins for medium or until cooked to your liking. Transfer lamb to a plate and cover with foil. Set aside for 20 mins to rest.
- Meanwhile, layer leek, sweet potato and garlic in an oiled medium disposable tray. Season

well. Pour over cream and sprinkle with cheese. Cover with greased foil. Bake in covered barbecue using indirect heat, or in oven, removing foil halfway through cooking, for the last 1 hour 15 mins of lamb cooking time or until vegetables are tender and cheese is golden.
- Serve lamb with sweet potato gratin and salad leaves.

3. Bean And Potato Bake, 4 Ways Recipe

Serving: 4 | Prep: 30mins | Ready in: 95mins

Ingredients

- 250ml (1 cup) vegetable stock
- 250ml (1 cup) milk
- 250ml (1 cup) milk
- 60ml (1/4 cup) thickened cream
- 1 garlic clove, thinly sliced
- 300g can Heinz Baked Beanz in tomato sauce
- 120g (1 1/2 cups) coarsely grated cheddar
- 600g Carisma potatoes, peeled
- Fresh herbs, to serve
- 1 chorizo sausage, skin removed, finely chopped
- 1/2 red onion, finely chopped
- 1/2 yellow capsicum, deseeded, finely chopped
- 1/2 tsp smoked paprika
- 2 short cut bacon rashers, cut into short thin strips
- 100g sour cream
- 1/2 bunch fresh chives, finely chopped
- 100g button mushrooms, thinly sliced
- 2 garlic cloves, crushed
- 2 fresh thyme sprigs
- 200g cooked chicken breast, shredded
- 45g (1/4 cup) drained sun-dried tomatoes
- 50g baby spinach, coarsely chopped

Direction

- Preheat oven to 190C/170C fan forced. Heat the stock, milk, cream and garlic in a saucepan over medium-low heat until mixture comes to a gentle simmer. Remove from heat then season.
- Place the baked beans, 1 cup cheddar and all the ingredients for your chosen potato bake in a large bowl.
- Use a mandoline to cut the potato into 2mm-thick slices.
- Transfer half the potato to the milk mixture and return to medium-low heat. Cook for 4-5 minutes or until potato starts to soften but not falling apart. Use a slotted spoon to drain potato of as much excess liquid as possible and transfer to the bowl with the bean mixture, reserving the milk mixture. Repeat with the remaining potato and reserved milk mixture. Carefully mix together the potato and bean mixture then transfer to a 7cm-deep, 11 x 21cm loaf pan or baking dish. Gently press down.
- Sprinkle the potato bake with the remaining cheddar. Bake for 1 hour or until the potatoes are golden and cooked through. Set aside for 10 minutes to cool slightly. Sprinkle with herbs to serve

4. Boulangerie Potatoes

Serving: 6 | Prep: 15mins | Ready in: 115mins

Ingredients

- 50g butter
- 3 brown onions, halved, thinly sliced
- 1.2kg Desiree potatoes, washed, thinly sliced (see note)
- 2 teaspoons fresh thyme leaves
- 500ml (2 cups) Massel chicken style liquid stock

Direction

- Melt half the butter in a medium frying pan over medium heat. Add the onion. Reduce

heat to low. Cook, stirring occasionally, for 20 minutes or until the onion is soft and slightly caramelized.
- Preheat oven to 180°C. Lightly rub a little of the remaining butter over the base and sides of a 2L (8-cup) capacity baking dish. Coarsely chop the remaining butter.
- Arrange a layer of potato, slightly overlapping, over the base of the dish. Top with a little of the caramelized onion and a little of the thyme. Continue layering with the remaining potato, caramelized onion and thyme, finishing with a layer of potato. Pour over the stock. Top with the chopped butter. Cover with baking paper and foil. Bake in oven for 1 hour.
- Uncover and bake for a further 20 minutes or until the potato is very soft and the top is golden. Set aside for 10 minutes to stand before serving.

Nutrition Information

- Calories: 227.05 calories
- Saturated Fat: 4.5 grams saturated fat
- Total Fat: 7.5 grams fat
- Total Carbohydrate: 3.5 grams carbohydrates
- Protein: 5 grams protein

5. Brie, Thyme And Bacon Dauphinoise Potato

Serving: 8 | Prep: 15mins | Ready in: 90mins

Ingredients

- 3 bacon rashers, thickly sliced
- 150g brie, thickly sliced
- 4 Carisma potatoes or washed potatoes, thinly sliced
- 1 brown onion, thinly sliced
- 2 garlic cloves, very thinly sliced
- 1 tablespoon thyme sprigs
- 300ml thickened cream
- 1/2 cup (125ml) chicken stock

Direction

- Preheat oven to 180C. Cook the bacon in a large frying pan over medium heat for 5 mins or until crisp.
- Reserve 4 of the brie slices. Layer potato, onion, bacon, garlic, thyme and remaining brie slices in a 6-cup (1.5L) ovenproof dish.
- Combine cream and stock in a jug. Season. Pour over potato mixture. Bake for 1 hour or until golden brown and tender. Top with reserved brie. Bake for 10 mins or until melted and golden. Set aside for 5 mins to rest.

Nutrition Information

- Calories: 331.732 calories
- Total Fat: 26 grams fat
- Saturated Fat: 15 grams saturated fat
- Total Carbohydrate: 12 grams carbohydrates
- Sugar: 3 grams sugar
- Protein: 10 grams protein
- Sodium: 502 milligrams sodium

6. Celeriac And Sweet Potato Bake

Serving: 0 | Prep: 25mins | Ready in: 105mins

Ingredients

- 1 cup cream
- 1 cup milk
- 2 garlic cloves, bruised
- 500g celeriac, peeled
- 500g sweet potato, peeled
- 1 brown onion, halved, thinly sliced
- 3 thick slices day-old Coles Bakery Pane Di Casa bread
- 1 tablespoon rosemary
- 1 tablespoon thyme leaves
- 30g butter, melted

Direction

- Preheat oven to 180C (160C fan-forced). Combine cream, milk and garlic in a small saucepan and bring to a simmer over low heat. Turn off heat and leave to infuse until needed.
- Cut celeriac into quarters then cut each piece crossways into slices about 5mm thick. Lightly grease a 5-cup capacity ovenproof dish. Layer the celeriac, sweet potato and onion neatly into the dish, finishing with celeriac.
- Remove the garlic from the cream mixture and reheat to a simmer. Stand the dish on a baking tray, and slowly pour cream over vegetables. Cover with a piece of non-stick baking paper, then foil. Bake for 1 hour, until vegetables are tender when pierced with a knife.
- Meanwhile, tear bread into pieces and place into a food processor. Process in short bursts until coarse crumbs form. Add herbs and butter and process until just combined. Uncover the dish and sprinkle crumb mixture over the vegetables. Return to oven and bake for 20 mins, or until golden brown.

7. Cheesy Bean And Potato Bake

Serving: 4 | Prep: 10mins | Ready in: 55mins

Ingredients

- 450g desiree potatoes, peeled, quartered
- 1/2 cup hot milk
- 3/4 cup grated tasty cheese
- 820g can baked beans in tomato sauce

Direction

- Preheat oven to 200°C/180°C fan-forced. Place potatoes in a medium saucepan. Cover with cold water. Season with salt. Bring to the boil over high heat. Boil for 15 minutes or until tender. Drain. Return potatoes to pan. Cook over low heat for 30 seconds or until dry. Remove from heat. Using a potato masher, coarsely mash potatoes. Add milk. Mash until smooth. Add 1/2 cup cheese. Stir until smooth. Season with salt and pepper.
- Place beans in a 5 cup-capacity baking dish. Cover with mash. Sprinkle with remaining cheese. Bake for 20 to 25 minutes or until golden and hot. Season with pepper. Serve.

Nutrition Information

- Calories: 337.946 calories
- Protein: 19 grams protein
- Total Fat: 10 grams fat
- Sugar: 13 grams sugar
- Cholesterol: 21 milligrams cholesterol
- Sodium: 912.61 milligrams sodium
- Saturated Fat: 6 grams saturated fat
- Total Carbohydrate: 37 grams carbohydrates

8. Cheesy Mashed Potato Bake

Serving: 4 | Prep: 10mins | Ready in: 45mins

Ingredients

- 800g sebago potatoes, peeled, roughly chopped
- 40g butter, chopped
- 1/4 cup milk, warmed
- 1 cup four cheese blend (see note)
- 2 green onions, thinly sliced
- 1/4 cup coarse fresh breadcrumbs
- 1/2 cup finely grated parmesan

Direction

- Place potato in a large saucepan. Cover with cold water. Bring to the boil over high heat. Cook for 10 to 15 minutes or until tender. Drain well.
- Return potato to pan over medium heat. Toss for 1 minute or until excess liquid has evaporated. Remove from heat. Mash until

smooth. Stir in butter, milk, 4-cheese blend and green onion until combined.
- Grease a 9cm-deep, 21cm-round (base) baking dish. Preheat grill on medium-high heat. Spoon mash into prepared dish. Smooth top. Sprinkle with breadcrumbs and parmesan. Season with pepper. Grill for 5 to 10 minutes or until top is golden and crunchy. Serve.

Nutrition Information

- Calories: 304.486 calories
- Total Fat: 16 grams fat
- Saturated Fat: 10.2 grams saturated fat
- Total Carbohydrate: 27 grams carbohydrates
- Sodium: 307 milligrams sodium
- Protein: 11.3 grams protein
- Cholesterol: 44 milligrams cholesterol

9. Cheesy Potato And Bacon 'lasagne'

Serving: 0 | Prep: 15mins | Ready in: 95mins

Ingredients

- 4 middle bacon rashers, rinds removed
- 1.5kg large sebago potatoes, peeled, sliced lengthways into 5mm-thick slices
- 200g (2 cups) coarsely grated mozzarella
- White pepper, to season
- 300ml carton pouring cream
- 125ml (1/2 cup) milk
- 2 eggs, lightly whisked

Direction

- Preheat oven to 170C/150C fan forced. Grease a 20cm-square baking dish with oil. Coarsely chop 3 bacon rashers. Reserve the remaining rasher. Place chopped bacon in a non-stick frying pan over medium-high heat. Cook, stirring occasionally, for 5 minutes, or until crisp.
- Place a layer of potatoes in the base of the prepared dish. Sprinkle over half the bacon and one-third of the cheese. Pour over one-quarter of the cream. Season with salt and white pepper. Top with another layer of potato, remaining bacon, half the remaining mozzarella and one-third of the remaining cream. Finish with a layer of potato.
- Whisk the milk, egg and remaining cream in a bowl. Season with salt and white pepper. Pour mixture over the potato and scatter with the remaining mozzarella. Cut the reserved bacon rasher into large pieces and arrange over the top of the cheese. Cover the dish with baking paper and foil. Bake for 55 minutes or until potato is nearly tender. Uncover and cook for another 15-20 minutes or until golden and bubbling. Stand for 10 minutes before serving.

10. Cheesy Potato Bake

Serving: 4 | Prep: 20mins | Ready in: 90mins

Ingredients

- 60g butter
- 1/4 cup plain flour
- 2 1/3 cups milk
- 2 cups grated tasty cheese
- 1.2kg Sebago potatoes, peeled, thinly sliced

Direction

- Preheat oven to 180°C. Grease a 6cm deep, 24cm square baking dish.
- Melt butter in a heavy-based saucepan over medium heat. Add flour. Cook, stirring constantly, for 2 minutes, or until bubbly. Remove from heat. Slowly add milk, stirring constantly until well combined. Return to heat. Cook, stirring, until sauce comes to the boil.
- Add 1 1/2 cups of cheese. Stir to combine.
- Arrange one-third of potatoes, overlapping slightly, over base of baking dish. Sprinkle with salt and pepper. Spoon one-third of the

cheese sauce over potatoes. Repeat twice. Sprinkle with remaining cheese. Bake for 1 hour, or until potatoes are tender and top is golden. If top begins to brown too much, cover with foil.

Nutrition Information

- Calories: 678.043 calories
- Protein: 29 grams protein
- Total Carbohydrate: 53 grams carbohydrates
- Sugar: 12 grams sugar
- Sodium: 550.97 milligrams sodium
- Total Fat: 38 grams fat
- Saturated Fat: 25 grams saturated fat

11. Cheesy Smashed Baked Potatoes

Serving: 6 | Prep: 10mins | Ready in: 50mins

Ingredients

- 1kg pkt Coles Australian Baby Red Royale Potatoes*
- 40g butter
- 2 tablespoons plain flour
- 1 cup (250ml) milk
- 1 cup (120g) coarsely grated vintage cheddar
- 2 teaspoons Dijon mustard
- 1/2 teaspoon smoked paprika
- 2 tablespoons finely chopped chives

Direction

- Preheat oven to 200°C. Line a baking tray with baking paper. Place potatoes on the lined tray. Spray with olive oil spray. Season. Roast, turning occasionally, for 30 mins or until tender.
- Meanwhile, melt the butter in a saucepan over medium heat. Add flour. Cook, stirring, for 1 min or until the mixture is grainy. Remove from heat. Add the milk and use a balloon whisk to whisk until well combined. Return to the heat. Cook, stirring, for 5 mins or until the sauce boils and thickens. Remove from heat. Add half the cheddar and stir to combine. Add mustard, paprika and chives. Stir to combine. Season.
- Use a small sharp knife to cut a small cross in the top of each potato. Cover with a clean tea towel and press down gently on each potato to open slightly. Spoon the sauce into the cuts. Sprinkle with remaining cheddar. Bake for 5-10 mins or until golden brown.

Nutrition Information

- Calories: 261.944 calories
- Saturated Fat: 8 grams saturated fat
- Protein: 11 grams protein
- Total Carbohydrate: 24 grams carbohydrates
- Sugar: 6 grams sugar
- Sodium: 308 milligrams sodium
- Total Fat: 13 grams fat

12. Colin's Potato Bake With Pancetta

Serving: 6 | Prep: 30mins | Ready in: 110mins

Ingredients

- 200g sliced pancetta or guanciale
- 20g butter
- 1 brown onion, thinly sliced
- 300ml pouring cream
- 1/2 bunch fresh thyme
- 3 garlic cloves, peeled, smashed
- 6 (about 1kg) Desiree potatoes
- 250g taleggio cheese, cut into 2cm pieces

Direction

- Coarsely chop half the pancetta. Tear remaining pancetta into pieces and set aside. Heat the butter in a 30cm (top measurement)

2L (8 cup) ovenproof frying pan over medium heat. Add onion and chopped pancetta. Cook, stirring often, for 8 minutes or until pancetta is crisp. Transfer mixture to a bowl. Rinse and dry the pan, then line with baking paper.
- Meanwhile, place the cream, thyme and garlic in a small saucepan. Bring to a simmer over medium heat. Set aside to infuse until required.
- Peel the potatoes and use a mandolin or sharp knife to slice to 2-3mm thick.
- Preheat oven to 180C/160C fan forced. Arrange one-fifth of the potato, slightly overlapping, evenly over the base of the prepared pan. Scatter with one-quarter of the onion mixture and one-fifth of the cheese. Repeat with 3 more layers, then a final layer of potato. Top with the torn pancetta and the remaining cheese.
- Strain the cream mixture over the layered potato mixture, reserving the thyme. Sprinkle with half the thyme. Cover with baking paper, then a layer of foil. Bake for 45 minutes. Remove paper and foil and bake for a further 25 minutes or until the potato is tender, pancetta is crisp and cheese is golden. Set aside for 10 minutes to firm before serving.

Nutrition Information

- Calories: 502.139 calories
- Saturated Fat: 23 grams saturated fat
- Total Carbohydrate: 21 grams carbohydrates
- Protein: 22 grams protein
- Total Fat: 37 grams fat

13. Creamy Celeriac And Potato Bake

Serving: 4 | Prep: 25mins | Ready in: 95mins

Ingredients

- 1 cup thickened cream
- 1/2 cup milk
- 4 garlic cloves, crushed
- 1 tablespoon fresh thyme leaves
- 850g celeriac, trimmed, peeled, very thinly sliced
- 2 (300g) desiree potatoes, peeled, very thinly sliced
- 150g blue shropshire cheese, crumbled (see note)

Direction

- Preheat oven to 200°C/180°C fan-forced. Grease a 6cm-deep, 16cm x 24cm (8 cup-capacity) oval baking dish.
- Combine cream, milk, garlic and thyme in large jug. Season with salt and pepper. Layer celeriac, potato and 3/4 of cheese in prepared dish. Pour over cream mixture. Lightly shake dish allowing cream mixture to settle between layers. Cover tightly with foil. Bake for 30 minutes.
- Remove foil. Top with remaining cheese. Bake for a further 30 to 40 minutes or until celeriac is tender. Stand for 10 minutes. Serve.

Nutrition Information

- Calories: 394.35 calories
- Protein: 14.1 grams protein
- Cholesterol: 75 milligrams cholesterol
- Sodium: 605 milligrams sodium
- Total Fat: 25.7 grams fat
- Saturated Fat: 16.2 grams saturated fat
- Total Carbohydrate: 20.9 grams carbohydrates

14. Creamy Dairy Free Curried Potato And Pumpkin Bake

Serving: 6 | Prep: 20mins | Ready in: 85mins

Ingredients

- 400g cauliflower, cut into small florets

- 270ml can coconut milk
- 1 tablespoon gluten-free Thai red curry paste
- 500g butternut pumpkin, thinly sliced
- 500g desiree potatoes, peeled, thinly sliced
- 125g can chickpeas, drained, rinsed
- Olive oil spray
- Fresh coriander leaves, to serve

Direction

- Place cauliflower in a large heatproof bowl. Add 1 tablespoon water. Cover loosely with plastic wrap. Microwave on HIGH (100%) for 5 minutes or until very tender. Drain. Transfer mixture to a food processor. Add coconut milk and curry paste. Process until smooth.
- Preheat oven to 200C/180C fan-forced. Grease a 4.5cm-deep, 16.5cm x 22cm (base) and 20.5cm x 26cm (top) baking dish.
- Place 1/3 of the pumpkin and potato, slightly overlapping, over base of prepared dish. Drizzle with 1/2 of the coconut mixture. Top with 1/2 the remaining pumpkin and potato, slightly overlapping. Drizzle with remaining coconut mixture. Top with remaining pumpkin and potato, slightly overlapping. Sprinkle with chickpeas. Spray with oil. Cover with baking paper, then foil.
- Bake for 40 minutes. Uncover. Bake for a further 20 minutes or until golden. Stand for 10 minutes. Serve sprinkled with coriander.

Nutrition Information

- Calories: 198.131 calories
- Saturated Fat: 6.8 grams saturated fat
- Total Carbohydrate: 18.1 grams carbohydrates
- Cholesterol: 1 milligrams cholesterol
- Sodium: 215 milligrams sodium
- Total Fat: 9.7 grams fat
- Protein: 6.5 grams protein

15. Creamy Kale, Pumpkin And Potato Bake

Serving: 0 | Prep: 20mins | Ready in: 100mins

Ingredients

- 300ml pouring cream
- 2 teaspoons vegetable stock powder
- 2 tablespoons olive oil
- 70g chopped kale
- 1 leek, halved lengthways, sliced
- 2 garlic cloves, crushed
- 1/2 (about 650g) butternut pumpkin, peeled, deseeded, cut into 5mm-thick slices
- 500g desiree potatoes, peeled, cut into 4mm-thick slices
- 400g can lentils, rinsed, drained
- 130g (1 1/4 cups) grated 3 cheese blend

Direction

- Preheat the oven to 200C/180C fan forced. Grease a 20 x 30cm baking dish. Combine the cream and stock powder in a jug and set aside.
- Heat 1 tablespoon oil in a large, deep frying pan over medium heat. Reserve a large handful of chopped kale. Add the remaining kale and 1 tbsp. water to the pan. Cook, stirring often, for 1-2 minutes or until the kale has wilted and the water has evaporated. Transfer to a bowl.
- Heat the remaining 1 tablespoon oil in the pan. Add the leek and garlic and cook, stirring, for 2 minutes or until soft. Add to the wilted kale. Cut each slice of pumpkin into 4-5cm pieces.
- Arrange a layer of sliced potato over the base of the prepared dish, overlapping slightly. Season. Top with half the kale mixture, then half the lentils. Drizzle with a little cream mixture. Top with a layer of pumpkin. Cover with the remaining kale mixture, then remaining lentils, seasoning as you layer. Drizzle with a little cream mixture. Finish with a layer of the remaining potato and pumpkin. Pour over the remaining cream mixture. Cover dish with foil and bake for 1 hour.

- Uncover the dish and top with the reserved kale. Scatter with cheese. Bake, uncovered, for 20 minutes or until golden. Stand for 10 minutes before serving.

16. Creamy Mashed Potato And Chive Bake

Serving: 8 | Prep: 15mins | Ready in: 70mins

Ingredients

- 2kg Sebago potatoes, peeled, halved
- 80g butter, softened
- 250g cream cheese, softened
- 1 cup milk
- 1/4 cup fresh chives, chopped
- 1/2 cup gruyere cheese, grated

Direction

- Grease an 8-cup-capacity ceramic baking dish. Preheat oven to 200C/ 180C fan-forced.
- Place potato in a large saucepan. Cover with cold water. Bring to the boil over high heat. Cook for 20 minutes or until tender. Drain. Return potato to pan. Toss over low heat for 1 to 2 minutes or until any excess water has evaporated.
- Using a potato masher, mash potato until smooth. Add butter and cream cheese. Mash to combine. Gradually stir in milk. Add chives. Season with salt and pepper. Stir to combine.
- Spoon potato into prepared baking dish. Top with cheese. Bake for 30 minutes or until golden and top is crisp. Serve.

Nutrition Information

- Calories: 374.752 calories
- Saturated Fat: 14.9 grams saturated fat
- Total Carbohydrate: 30.2 grams carbohydrates
- Protein: 10.4 grams protein
- Cholesterol: 57 milligrams cholesterol
- Sodium: 256 milligrams sodium
- Total Fat: 22.3 grams fat

17. Creamy Potato And Ham Bake With Fresh Rosemary

Serving: 6 | Prep: 15mins | Ready in: 85mins

Ingredients

- Olive oil, to grease
- 1.2kg red rascal potatoes, peeled, thinly sliced
- 150g sliced ham, cut into thin strips
- 300ml extra light thickened cream
- 100ml milk
- 140g (1/2 cup) shredded parmesan
- 1 large sprig fresh rosemary, leaves picked

Direction

- Preheat oven to 180°C. Brush a 2L (8-cup) capacity baking dish with olive oil to grease. Arrange one-quarter of the potato, slightly overlapping, over the base of the prepared dish. Top with one-third of the ham. Continue layering with remaining potato and ham, finishing with a layer of potato.
- Place the cream and milk in a small saucepan over medium-high heat. Bring just to the boil. Pour over the potato mixture. Cover with foil and bake in oven for 30 minutes. Uncover and bake in oven for 20 minutes.
- Top with the parmesan and rosemary. Bake in oven for a further 20 minutes or until potato is tender. Set aside for 5 minutes to stand. Serve

Nutrition Information

- Calories: 363.519 calories
- Sugar: 6 grams sugar
- Cholesterol: 62 milligrams cholesterol
- Total Carbohydrate: 25 grams carbohydrates
- Protein: 20 grams protein
- Sodium: 720.61 milligrams sodium

- Total Fat: 20 grams fat
- Saturated Fat: 12 grams saturated fat

18. Creamy Potato And Kale Gratin

Serving: 8 | Prep: 40mins | Ready in: 135mins

Ingredients

- 1/2 bunch kale
- 1 tablespoon extra virgin olive oil
- 1 brown onion, halved, thinly sliced
- 2 garlic cloves, crushed
- 2 teaspoons fresh thyme leaves, chopped
- 1.5kg red delight potatoes, very thinly sliced (see Notes)
- 300ml pure cream
- 3/4 cup cheddar, grated
- 50g blue cheese, crumbled
- 1/4 cup pecans, roughly chopped
- Extra fresh thyme leaves, to serve

Direction

- Trim and discard stems and center vein of kale. Roughly chop leaves.
- Heat oil in a large frying pan over medium heat. Add onion. Cook for 5 minutes or until golden. Add garlic, thyme and kale. Cook, stirring, for 2 to 3 minutes or until kale is wilted.
- Preheat oven to 200C/180C fan-forced. Grease a 10-cup-capacity metal baking pan.
- Layer 1/3 of the potato over base of prepared pan. Spoon over 1/2 the onion mixture, spreading evenly. Arrange 1/2 the remaining potato on top. Repeat layers. Pour over cream. Season with salt and pepper. Cover tightly with foil. Bake for 1 hour or until potato is tender.
- Remove and discard foil. Sprinkle over combined cheddar, blue cheese and pecans. Bake for a further 20 to 25 minutes or until golden and tender. Stand for 10 minutes. Sprinkle with extra thyme. Serve.

Nutrition Information

- Calories: 409.885 calories
- Total Fat: 26.6 grams fat
- Cholesterol: 55 milligrams cholesterol
- Sodium: 207 milligrams sodium
- Saturated Fat: 13.7 grams saturated fat
- Total Carbohydrate: 29.4 grams carbohydrates
- Protein: 11 grams protein

19. Creamy Potato And Nutmeg Bake

Serving: 6 | Prep: 10mins | Ready in: 70mins

Ingredients

- 1kg desiree, pontiac or pink-eye potatoes, peeled, thinly sliced
- 375ml (1 1/2 cups) thickened cream
- 80ml (1/3 cup) dry white wine
- 2 eggs, lightly whisked
- 45g (1/2 cup) shredded parmesan
- 2 garlic cloves, crushed
- Pinch of salt
- 40g (1/2 cup) coarsely grated cheddar
- Pinch of ground nutmeg

Direction

- Preheat oven to 180°C. Arrange potato over the base of a rectangular 2L (8-cup) capacity ovenproof ceramic dish.
- Use a balloon whisk to whisk the cream, wine, egg, half the parmesan, garlic and salt together in a large jug. Pour the cream mixture over the potatoes. Sprinkle with the combined remaining parmesan and cheddar, then sprinkle with nutmeg.
- Cook, covered, in preheated oven for 45 minutes or until the potato is tender. Uncover and cook for a further 15 minutes or until the cheese melts and is golden. Serve immediately.

Nutrition Information

- Calories: 415.143 calories
- Total Fat: 30 grams fat
- Saturated Fat: 18 grams saturated fat
- Sugar: 4 grams sugar
- Protein: 12 grams protein
- Total Carbohydrate: 23 grams carbohydrates
- Sodium: 226.75 milligrams sodium

20. Creamy Potato And Rosemary Bake

Serving: 4 | Prep: 30mins | Ready in: 71mins

Ingredients

- 6 large (1kg) coliban potatoes
- 2 teaspoons dijon mustard
- 1/2 cup pure cream
- 1 egg yolk
- 1 tablespoon fresh rosemary leaves
- 1/2 cup grated gruyere cheese

Direction

- Using a fork, pierce each potato 5 times. Place potatoes, evenly spaced, around a large, microwave-safe plate. Microwave on HIGH (100%) for 5 to 6 minutes or until just tender. Carefully remove plate from microwave. Set aside until cool enough to handle. Cut potatoes into 1cm-thick slices.
- Preheat oven to 180°C/160°C fan-forced. Grease a 5cm-deep, 21cm (base), round pie dish. Place mustard, cream and egg yolk in a jug. Season with salt and pepper. Whisk to combine.
- Arrange one-third potato, slightly overlapping, over base of prepared dish. Sprinkle with one-third rosemary leaves and one-third cheese. Repeat layers twice more with remaining potato, rosemary and cheese. Pour cream mixture over potato mixture layers. Bake for 35 minutes or until potatoes are cooked through and cheese is melted and golden. Stand for 10 minutes. Serve.

Nutrition Information

- Calories: 372.84 calories
- Total Fat: 19.7 grams fat
- Cholesterol: 102 milligrams cholesterol
- Saturated Fat: 11.9 grams saturated fat
- Total Carbohydrate: 34.2 grams carbohydrates
- Protein: 11.5 grams protein
- Sodium: 150 milligrams sodium

21. Creamy Potato Bacon Bake

Serving: 6 | Prep: 15mins | Ready in: 75mins

Ingredients

- 6 pontiac potatoes, thinly sliced
- 1 brown onion, thinly sliced
- 3 bacon rashers, finely chopped
- 2 garlic cloves, crushed
- 1 1/2 cups (375ml) thickened cream
- 1/2 cup (125ml) Massel chicken style liquid stock

Direction

- Preheat oven to 180°c. Grease a 1 1/2-litre (6 cup) capacity deep baking dish with melted butter. Layer the potato, onion and bacon in the prepared dish.
- Combine the garlic, cream and chicken stock in a large saucepan over high heat. Bring to a simmer. Remove from heat and pour evenly over the potato mixture. Bake in preheated oven for 1 hour or until tender. Remove from heat. Set aside for 5 minutes to cool slightly before serving.

Nutrition Information

- Calories: 403.91 calories
- Sugar: 4 grams sugar
- Protein: 9 grams protein
- Total Fat: 31 grams fat
- Saturated Fat: 18 grams saturated fat
- Total Carbohydrate: 21 grams carbohydrates
- Sodium: 420.74 milligrams sodium

22. Creamy Potato Bake

Serving: 6 | Prep: 20mins | Ready in: 110mins

Ingredients

- 1 1/2 kg brushed potatoes, peeled and thinly sliced
- 3 cloves garlic, thinly sliced
- 1 tablespoon fresh thyme leaves
- 1 cup milk
- 300ml thin cream
- 30g butter, melted
- 2 tablespoon finely grated parmesan
- 2 onions, halved, thinly sliced

Direction

- Preheat oven to 180C or 160C fan-forced. Lightly grease a 7-cup ovenproof dish. Layer 1/3 of potatoes over base. Top with half the onion, garlic and thyme. Season with salt and pepper. Pour over 1/3 of combined milk and cream.
- Repeat layers. Finish with remaining potato and pour remaining milk and cream over. Brush a sheet of foil with oil and place oil-side down over the potato. Seal tightly. Bake for 45 mins. Uncover and brush top with melted butter. Cook a further 45 mins until tender and golden brown. Sprinkle with parmesan for last 15 mins of cooking.

23. Creamy Scalloped Potato Bake With Pesto And Rocket

Serving: 0 | Prep: 10mins | Ready in: 80mins

Ingredients

- 10g butter
- 200ml Bulla Crème Fraîche
- 800g desiree potatoes, thinly sliced
- 1 onion, thinly sliced
- 50g baby rocket leaves, to serve
- Basil pesto, (homemade or store-bought) to serve

Direction

- Preheat oven to 200C (180C fan forced). Generously grease a 6cm deep, 15cm x 24cm (base) ovenproof dish with butter. Combine crème fraiche salt and pepper in a jug and mix well.
- Arrange a layer of potatoes over base of prepared dish. Top with a layer of onion. Drizzle with a little cream mixture. Repeat layers until all ingredients have been used.
- Cover dish tightly with foil. Bake for 40 to 50 minutes or until potatoes are just tender. Remove foil. Cook for a further 20 minutes or until top is golden.
- Serve at the table topped with rocket and a generous drizzle of pesto.

24. Creamy Scalloped Potato Tray Bake Recipe

Serving: 6 | Prep: 25mins | Ready in: 80mins

Ingredients

- 2 cups thickened cream
- 2 garlic cloves, crushed
- 4 large red potatoes, very thinly sliced
- 2 teaspoons fresh thyme leaves
- 2/3 cup grated 3 cheese blend (see note)

Direction

- Preheat oven to 220C/200C fan-forced. Grease a 3.5cm-deep, 21cm x 30cm baking tray.
- Place cream and garlic in a microwave-safe jug. Microwave on HIGH (100%) for 1 minute 30 seconds or until warm.
- Meanwhile, arrange half the potato, in layers and slightly overlapping, in prepared tray. Sprinkle with half the thyme and cheese. Season with salt and pepper.
- Pour over half the cream mixture. Arrange remaining potato, in layers and slightly overlapping, on top. Pour over remaining cream mixture. Cover tightly with foil. Bake for 30 to 35 minutes or until potato is just tender.
- Uncover. Sprinkle with remaining thyme and cheese. Season with salt and pepper. Bake for a further 15 to 20 minutes or until golden and potato is tender. Serve.

Nutrition Information

- Calories: 438.565 calories
- Total Fat: 34.8 grams fat
- Total Carbohydrate: 20.6 grams carbohydrates
- Sodium: 175 milligrams sodium
- Saturated Fat: 22.7 grams saturated fat
- Protein: 9.1 grams protein

25. Crispy Garlic And Thyme Boulangere Potatoes

Serving: 8 | Prep: 20mins | Ready in: 95mins

Ingredients

- 2.4kg large oval sebago potatoes, peeled
- 1 tablespoon fresh thyme leaves, plus extra small sprigs to serve
- 3 garlic cloves, peeled, halved
- 1/3 cup extra virgin olive oil
- 1 teaspoon cracked black pepper
- 2 teaspoons chicken-style stock powder
- 1/3 cup hot water
- 1 teaspoon sea salt
- 1/4 cup finely grated parmesan

Direction

- Preheat oven to 200C/180C fan-forced. Grease a 4cm-deep, 18cm x 28cm (base) roasting pan.
- Using the slicing blade attachment on a food processor, slice potato lengthways into 2mm-thick slices. Transfer to a large bowl.
- Carefully remove slicing attachment. Place the thyme and garlic in a small food processor. Process until finely chopped. Add oil. Process until well combined. Pour over the potato in bowl. Add pepper. Toss well to coat. Arrange potato slices, standing upright, in 2 rows in prepared pan.
- Blend stock powder with hot water until dissolved. Pour along the centre of the 2 rows of potato. Sprinkle potato with salt. Cover tightly with foil. Bake for 30 minutes. Remove and discard foil. Bake for a further 40 to 45 minutes or until potato is tender and top is golden and crispy.
- Sprinkle top of potato with the parmesan and extra thyme. Stand for 5 minutes. Serve.

Nutrition Information

- Calories: 270.309 calories
- Sodium: 476 milligrams sodium
- Saturated Fat: 1.9 grams saturated fat
- Total Fat: 10.6 grams fat
- Total Carbohydrate: 33.4 grams carbohydrates
- Protein: 7.1 grams protein

26. Crispy Topped Potato Bake

Serving: 0 | Prep: 30mins | Ready in: 125mins

Ingredients

- 75g butter, chopped
- 60ml (1/4 cup) pouring cream
- 2 tablespoons extra virgin olive oil
- 2 garlic cloves, bruised
- 4 sprigs fresh lemon thyme
- 2 dried bay leaves
- 2.4kg Red Delight potatoes, peeled
- 1 teaspoon sea salt flakes

Direction

- Preheat oven to 180°C. Grease a 2.5L baking dish with melted butter.
- Stir the butter, cream, oil, garlic, thyme and bay leaves in a small saucepan over medium-low heat for 2-3 minutes or until melted and smooth. Season with pepper.
- Use a mandolin or a sharp knife to cut the potatoes, 1 at a time, into 2mm-thick slices. Discard the end slices of each potato and place in stacks on a work surface. Arrange the slices standing on their sides, 1 stack at a time, in tightly packed rows in the prepared dish.
- Strain the butter mixture through a small sieve into a jug. Discard solids. Pour butter mixture evenly over the potato. Sprinkle with salt. Cover with foil and bake for 30 minutes. Remove foil and bake for a further 1 hour or until top is golden and crisp. Set aside for 10 minutes to cool slightly.

Nutrition Information

- Calories: 249.755 calories
- Total Fat: 13 grams fat
- Saturated Fat: 6.5 grams saturated fat
- Total Carbohydrate: 28 grams carbohydrates
- Protein: 5.5 grams protein

27. Double Cheese Sweet Potato Bake Recipe

Serving: 6 | Prep: 15mins | Ready in: 85mins

Ingredients

- 500g desiree potatoes, thinly sliced
- 500g orange sweet potatoes, thinly sliced
- 1 bunch fresh sage
- 1 large eschalot, finely chopped
- 2 garlic cloves, finely chopped
- 100g goat's cheese, crumbled
- 1 cup grated cheddar
- 1 1/2 cups light thickened cream for cooking
- 1 tablespoon chopped pecans

Direction

- Preheat oven to 200C/180C fan-forced. Grease a 6-cup-capacity oval baking dish.
- Place half the potato and sweet potato, in layers and slightly overlapping, over base of prepared dish. Tear half the sage. Sprinkle potato with torn sage, half the eschalot, half the garlic and half the cheeses. Drizzle with half the cream. Season with salt and pepper. Arrange remaining potato and sweet potato, in layers and slightly overlapping, over the top. Drizzle with remaining cream. Sprinkle with remaining eschalot, garlic and cheeses. Season with salt and pepper. Cover tightly with foil. Bake for 40 minutes.
- Uncover. Bake for a further 25 minutes or until golden and tender. Sprinkle with pecans and remaining sage leaves. Bake for a further 5 minutes or until sage is crisp. Stand for 10 minutes. Serve.

Nutrition Information

- Calories: 398.413 calories
- Saturated Fat: 15.1 grams saturated fat
- Sodium: 284 milligrams sodium
- Protein: 14.4 grams protein
- Cholesterol: 61 milligrams cholesterol
- Total Fat: 24.3 grams fat
- Total Carbohydrate: 26 grams carbohydrates

28. Easy Cheese And Tomato Potato Bake

Serving: 4 | Prep: 10mins | Ready in: 40mins

Ingredients

- 400g can lentils, drained, rinsed
- 525g jar Heinz Tomato and Garlic Bolognese Pasta Sauce
- 1 green onion, thinly sliced
- 2 tablespoons chopped fresh flat-leaf parsley leaves
- 1kg Sebago potatoes, peeled, very thinly sliced
- 1 1/2 cups grated tasty cheese
- 1/4 cup finely grated parmesan (or vegetarian hard cheese)
- Chopped fresh flat-leaf parsley, to serve

Direction

- Preheat oven to 180C/160C fan-forced. Grease a 5cm-deep, 20cm x 26cm roasting pan.
- Combine lentils, pasta sauce, onion and parsley in a large bowl. Season with salt and pepper.
- Layer 1/6 of the potato slices over the base of prepared pan. Top with 1/5 of the lentil mixture, spreading to cover. Repeat layering, finishing with a layer of potato. Sprinkle with cheeses. Cover tightly with baking paper, then foil. Bake for 1 hour.
- Remove and discard foil and paper. Bake for a further 20 to 25 minutes or until potato is tender and cheese is golden. Stand 10 minutes. Serve sprinkled with parsley.

29. Easy Creamy Potato Bake

Serving: 6 | Prep: 20mins | Ready in: 90mins

Ingredients

- 800g chat potatoes
- 50g butter
- 2 garlic cloves, crushed
- 2 teaspoons finely chopped fresh thyme leaves, plus extra sprigs to serve
- 1/4 cup plain flour
- 1 1/2 cups milk
- 125g cream cheese, chopped, softened
- 1 teaspoon dijon mustard
- 1 cup grated colby cheese

Direction

- Preheat oven to 200C/180C fan-forced. Grease a 5cm-deep, 16.5cm x 22cm (base) roasting pan.
- Place potato in a large saucepan. Cover with cold water. Bring to the boil over high heat. Reduce heat to medium. Simmer for 12 minutes or until just tender. Drain. Set aside for 10 minutes or until cool enough to handle. Cut into quarters.
- Meanwhile, melt butter in a saucepan over medium-high heat. Add garlic and thyme. Cook, stirring, for 30 seconds or until fragrant. Add flour. Cook, stirring, for 1 minute or until bubbling. Gradually add milk, stirring constantly, until mixture is smooth and combined. Cook, stirring, for 4 to 5 minutes or until mixture boils and thickens. Add cream cheese, mustard and 1/2 cup Colby cheese. Cook, stirring, for 1 to 2 minutes or until melted and smooth. Remove from heat.
- Add potato to cheese mixture. Season with salt and pepper. Stir to combine. Transfer mixture to prepared pan. Top with remaining Colby cheese. Bake for 30 to 40 minutes or until golden. Serve sprinkled with extra thyme.

Nutrition Information

- Calories: 363.758 calories
- Saturated Fat: 15.1 grams saturated fat
- Total Fat: 22.2 grams fat
- Total Carbohydrate: 25.1 grams carbohydrates
- Protein: 12.4 grams protein
- Cholesterol: 62 milligrams cholesterol
- Sodium: 364 milligrams sodium

30. Extreme Cheese Fondue Potato Pie

Serving: 0 | Prep: 15mins | Ready in: 75mins

Ingredients

- 1kg desiree potatoes
- 4 thick slices white bread, cut into 1cm pieces
- Fresh thyme leaves, to sprinkle
- 60g butter
- 1 garlic clove, crushed
- 40g (1/4 cup) plain flour
- 125ml (1/2 cup) white wine
- 500ml (2 cups) milk
- 80g (1 cup) coarsely grated gruyere
- 200g (2 cups) coarsely grated mozzarella

Direction

- Preheat the oven to 200C/180C fan forced. Line a large baking tray with baking paper. Use a mandoline or a sharp knife to carefully slice the potatoes into 2mm-thick slices.
- Scatter the potato slices in a single layer over the prepared tray (it's okay if they overlap slightly). Spray lightly with olive oil and bake for 30 minutes or until golden and crisp around the edges.
- Meanwhile, to make the cheesy fondue sauce, place the butter and garlic in a saucepan over medium heat until the butter is foaming. Add the flour and cook, stirring, for 1-2 minutes or until mixture bubbles. Remove from heat. Add the wine and stir until smooth. Gradually stir in the milk. Stir over medium heat for 2 minutes or until the sauce has thickened. Stir in the cheeses and stir until smooth. Season.
- Lightly grease a large baking dish. Spread half of the cheese sauce over the base of the dish. Reserve about 20 of the potato slices. Place the remaining slices, slightly overlapping, on top of the sauce. Spread with the remaining sauce. Arrange the reserved potato slices around the edge of the dish and scatter over the bread. Spray lightly with olive oil. Bake for 15-20 minutes or until the bread is golden and the cheese sauce is bubbling. Scatter with the thyme.

31. Fennel And Potato Gratin

Serving: 4 | Prep: 20mins | Ready in: 80mins

Ingredients

- 400g desiree potatoes, peeled, thinly sliced
- 1 medium fennel bulb, trimmed, thinly sliced
- 1 small brown onion, thinly sliced
- 1/3 cup fresh breadcrumbs
- 2 tablespoons finely grated parmesan
- 1/2 cup Massel chicken style liquid stock

Direction

- Preheat oven to 180°C/160°C fan-forced. Lightly grease a 6 cup-capacity baking dish.
- Layer one quarter potato over base of prepared dish. Top with one-third fennel and onion. Repeat layers, finishing with potato.
- Combine breadcrumbs and parmesan in a bowl. Pour stock over potato mixture. Sprinkle breadcrumb mixture. Bake for 45 to 50 minutes or until potato is tender and breadcrumb mixture. Stand for 5 minutes. Serve.

Nutrition Information

- Calories: 120.695 calories
- Saturated Fat: 0.7 grams saturated fat
- Total Carbohydrate: 19 grams carbohydrates
- Cholesterol: 19 milligrams cholesterol
- Sodium: 273 milligrams sodium
- Total Fat: 1.5 grams fat
- Protein: 5.6 grams protein

32. Garlic And Rosemary Potato Bake

Serving: 6 | Prep: 15mins | Ready in: 75mins

Ingredients

- 1kg brushed potatoes, peeled
- 4 garlic cloves, thinly sliced
- 1/4 cup rosemary leaves
- 40g butter, melted
- 1/2 cup (125ml) chicken stock
- 1/4 cup (20g) finely grated parmesan
- Rosemary leaves, extra, to serve

Direction

- Preheat oven to 220°C. Lightly grease a shallow 6-cup (1.5L) ovenproof dish.
- Use a sharp knife or mandolin to carefully cut potatoes crossways into 3mm-thick slices. Line the base of the prepared dish with a single layer of potato slices, overlapping slightly. Sprinkle with one-quarter of the garlic and rosemary. Brush with a little of the melted butter. Continue layering with remaining potato slices, garlic, rosemary and butter. Drizzle with stock. Cover dish tightly with foil. Bake for 25 mins.
- Reduce oven to 180°C. Remove the foil. Bake, uncovered, for 30-35 mins or until potato is tender and top is golden and crisp. Serve sprinkled with parmesan and extra rosemary.

33. Garlic And Rosemary Scalloped Potatoes

Serving: 6 | Prep: 30mins | Ready in: 90mins

Ingredients

- 1.5kg desiree potatoes
- 4 garlic cloves, thinly sliced
- 1 tablespoon rosemary leaves, finely chopped
- 1/2 cup (125ml) thin cream
- 1/2 cup (125ml) Massel chicken style liquid stock
- 2 teaspoons whole rosemary leaves

Direction

- Preheat the oven to 200°C. Lightly grease a rectangular ovenproof dish (approximately 29 x 19 x 5cm deep). Peel the potatoes and cut into slices about 3-5mm thick.
- Arrange one-third of the potato into a layer in the base of the dish. Sprinkle half the garlic and rosemary over the potato. Repeat another layer of potato, the remaining garlic and chopped rosemary, then a final layer of potato slices.
- Combine the cream and stock in a jug, and whisk with a fork to combine. Drizzle over the top of the potatoes. Season with freshly ground black pepper, and scatter the whole rosemary leaves on top.
- Cover tightly with foil and bake for 30 minutes, until the potatoes are just tender. Remove the foil and cook for another 30 minutes, until the top is golden brown. Stand for 5 minutes, then cut into rectangles to serve.

Nutrition Information

- Calories: 231.591 calories
- Saturated Fat: 5 grams saturated fat
- Sugar: 3 grams sugar
- Protein: 6 grams protein
- Sodium: 103.81 milligrams sodium
- Total Fat: 8 grams fat
- Total Carbohydrate: 31 grams carbohydrates

34. Garlic And Thyme Scalloped Potatoes

Serving: 4 | Prep: 30mins | Ready in: 105mins

Ingredients

- 10g butter, melted
- 800g desiree potatoes, peeled
- 2 garlic cloves, crushed
- 2 tablespoons fresh thyme leaves
- 300ml pure cream

Direction

- Preheat oven to 200°C/180°C fan-forced. Brush a 6cm-deep, 19cm x 20cm (base) baking dish with butter. Thinly slice potatoes.
- Place one-third of potato, slightly overlapping, over base of prepared dish. Sprinkle with one-third of the garlic and thyme. Arrange half the remaining potato over garlic and thyme. Sprinkle with half the remaining garlic and thyme. Repeat with remaining potato, garlic and thyme. Drizzle with cream. Season with salt and pepper. Cover tightly with foil.
- Bake for 35 to 40 minutes or until just tender. Remove foil. Bake for 30 to 35 minutes or until golden. Serve.

Nutrition Information

- Calories: 471.308 calories
- Total Fat: 34.8 grams fat
- Saturated Fat: 22.8 grams saturated fat
- Total Carbohydrate: 29 grams carbohydrates
- Cholesterol: 109 milligrams cholesterol
- Sodium: 83 milligrams sodium
- Protein: 6.5 grams protein

35. Ham And Leek Potato Gratin Recipe

Serving: 6 | Prep: 10mins | Ready in: 70mins

Ingredients

- 8 brushed potatoes, washed, thinly sliced
- 100g thickly sliced ham, chopped
- 2 garlic cloves, thinly sliced
- 1 brown onion, thinly sliced
- 1 leek, pale section only, thinly sliced
- 1 tbs thyme sprigs
- 1 cup (120g) coarsely grated cheddar
- 1/2 cup (125ml) thickened cream
- 1/3 cup (80g) sour cream
- 1/4 cup (60ml) chicken stock

Direction

- Preheat oven to 180°C. Grease a 6-cup (1.5L) ovenproof dish. Arrange one-third of the potato in the prepared dish. Top with half the ham, garlic, onion, leek and thyme. Sprinkle with one-third of the cheddar. Continue layering with remaining potato, ham, garlic, onion, leek, thyme and cheddar, finishing with the potato and cheddar.
- Combine the cream, sour cream and stock in a jug. Season. Carefully pour the cream mixture over the potato mixture in the dish.
- Bake for 1 hour or until the sauce thickens and the potato is golden brown and tender.
- Set the potato gratin aside for 10 mins to rest before serving.

Nutrition Information

- Calories: 617.576 calories
- Total Fat: 29 grams fat
- Saturated Fat: 18 grams saturated fat
- Sugar: 7 grams sugar
- Protein: 23 grams protein
- Sodium: 734 milligrams sodium
- Total Carbohydrate: 58 grams carbohydrates

36. Hash Brown Potato Bake Recipe

Serving: 8 | Prep: 20mins | Ready in: 70mins

Ingredients

- 1.5kg brushed potatoes, peeled, coarsely grated

- 60g butter, melted
- 80ml (1/3 cup) cream
- 80g (1 cup) grated cheddar

Direction

- Preheat oven to 190C/170C fan forced. Place potato in a colander and use your hands to squeeze out the excess moisture. Transfer the potato to a large bowl. Add the butter and cream. Season and stir well to combine.
- Transfer the potato mixture to an 18 x 28cm baking pan and press in firmly. Smooth the surface. Cover tightly with foil and place pan on a large baking tray. Bake for 30 minutes.
- Remove the foil and sprinkle over the cheese. Bake for a further 20 minutes or until the potato is tender and the cheese is golden. Set aside for 10 minutes, before cutting into slices to serve.

37. Hayden Quinn's Ultimate Sweet Potato Bake Recipe

Serving: 4 | Prep: 0S | Ready in:

Ingredients

- 2 tbs olive or macadamia oil
- 3 lean rashers bacon, roughly chopped
- 600g sweet potato, very thinly sliced
- 1 cup (240g) ricotta
- 1 cup (250ml) coconut milk
- 1 tsp ground nutmeg

Direction

- Preheat oven to 200°C and lightly grease an 8-cup capacity ovenproof dish. Heat the oil in a large fry pan over medium heat. Add the bacon and cook, stirring occasionally, until browned. Remove from pan and set aside.
- In batches, add the sweet potato slices to the fry pan and cook for 2 minutes each side or until lightly golden. Transfer the bacon and the sweet potato to the ovenproof dish.
- Place the ricotta, coconut milk and nutmeg in a bowl and whisk until smooth. Season with salt. Pour over the sweet potato and bacon mixture.
- Transfer to the oven and bake for 20-25 minutes, until lightly golden on top. Serve immediately.

38. Healthier Potato And Sweet Potato Bake

Serving: 6 | Prep: 20mins | Ready in: 110mins

Ingredients

- 50g margarine spread
- 1/4 cup plain flour
- 375ml can light and creamy evaporated milk
- 500g Carisma potatoes, unpeeled, cut into 2mm-thick slices
- 1kg orange sweet potato, unpeeled, cut into 2mm-thick slices
- 2 tablespoons chopped fresh sage leaves
- 2 garlic cloves, crushed
- 1/4 cup finely grated parmesan (or vegetarian hard cheese)
- 2 tablespoons seed mix (pepitas and sunflower seeds)

Direction

- Preheat oven to 200C/180C fan-forced. Grease a 6cm-deep, 20cm x 28cm oval roasting pan.
- Melt margarine in a saucepan over medium-high heat. Add flour. Cook, stirring, for 1 minute or until bubbling. Gradually add milk, stirring until smooth and combined. Cook, stirring constantly, for 4 to 5 minutes or until mixture boils and thickens. Season well with salt and pepper. Pour into base of prepared dish.
- Place potato, sweet potato, sage and garlic in a large bowl. Toss to combine. Arrange potato

slices, standing upright, in prepared dish, alternating between varieties. Spoon remaining garlic and sage mixture between potato slices. Sprinkle with parmesan (or vegetarian hard cheese) and seed mix. Season with salt and pepper.
- Cover with baking paper, then foil. Bake for 50 minutes. Uncover. Bake for a further 30 to 35 minutes or until golden and tender. Stand for 10 minutes. Serve.

Nutrition Information

- Calories: 348.94 calories
- Total Fat: 10.6 grams fat
- Saturated Fat: 3.7 grams saturated fat
- Total Carbohydrate: 45.3 grams carbohydrates
- Sodium: 275 milligrams sodium
- Protein: 14.1 grams protein
- Cholesterol: 11 milligrams cholesterol

39. Individual Creamy Potato Gratins

Serving: 2 | Prep: 10mins | Ready in: 55mins

Ingredients

- Melted butter, to grease
- 400g sebago (brushed) potatoes, peeled, thinly sliced
- 1 garlic clove, thinly sliced
- 160ml (2/3 cup) thickened cream
- Pinch of ground nutmeg

Direction

- Preheat oven to 220°C. Brush two 250ml (1-cup) capacity ovenproof dishes with melted butter to grease. Alternately layer the potatoes and garlic in the prepared dishes.
- Combine the cream and nutmeg in a medium jug. Season with salt and pepper. Pour the cream mixture evenly among the dishes. Bake in oven for 45 minutes or until tender. Serve.

Nutrition Information

- Calories: 449.32 calories
- Saturated Fat: 23 grams saturated fat
- Total Fat: 36 grams fat
- Total Carbohydrate: 26 grams carbohydrates
- Protein: 6.5 grams protein

40. Individual Pumpkin And Gnocchi Bakes

Serving: 4 | Prep: 10mins | Ready in: 35mins

Ingredients

- 600g butternut pumpkin, seeded, peeled, cut into 2cm cubes
- 500g potato gnocchi
- 200g baby spinach leaves
- 1 cup (120g) frozen peas
- 490g jar carbonara pasta sauce
- 1/2 cup (60g) grated tasty cheddar

Direction

- Preheat oven to 200C. Cook the pumpkin in a large saucepan of boiling water for 5-7 mins or until just tender. Drain well.
- Meanwhile, cook gnocchi in a large saucepan of boiling water following packet directions. Drain well.
- Combine the pumpkin, gnocchi, spinach, peas and carbonara sauce in a large bowl. Season. Spoon evenly among four 1 1/2 cup (375ml) ovenproof dishes. Place on a baking tray. Sprinkle evenly with cheddar. Bake for 10-15 mins or until golden brown and heated through.

Nutrition Information

- Calories: 488.516 calories
- Total Fat: 18 grams fat
- Total Carbohydrate: 58 grams carbohydrates
- Sugar: 14 grams sugar
- Saturated Fat: 10 grams saturated fat
- Protein: 18 grams protein

41. Janssons Frestelse (Jansson's Temptation)

Serving: 8 | Prep: 30mins | Ready in: 100mins

Ingredients

- Melted butter, to grease
- 1.5kg potatoes, peeled
- 1 tablespoon olive oil
- 80g butter, chopped
- 3 brown onions, halved, thinly sliced
- 1 x 80g btl anchovy fillets, drained, finely chopped
- Ground white pepper
- 250ml (1 cup) thickened cream
- 250ml (1 cup) milk
- 70g (1 cup) fresh breadcrumbs (made from day-old bread)

Direction

- Preheat oven to 180°C. Brush a 2L (8-cup) capacity baking dish with melted butter to lightly grease. Cut the potatoes into 3mm-thick slices. Cut each slice into 3mm-thick matchsticks. Place in a large bowl of cold water to prevent browning.
- Heat the oil and half the butter in a medium frying pan over medium heat. Add the onion and cook, stirring occasionally, for 10 minutes or until soft.
- Drain the potato and pat dry with paper towel. Place one-fifth of the potato over the base of the prepared dish. Top with one-quarter of the onion and one-quarter of the anchovy. Season with white pepper. Continue layering with the remaining potato, onion, anchovy and pepper, finishing with potato.
- Heat the cream and milk in a medium saucepan over medium heat until mixture comes to a simmer. Pour the cream mixture over the potato mixture. Top with the breadcrumbs and remaining butter.
- Cover with non-stick baking paper and foil. Bake for 30 minutes. Remove the paper and foil. Cook for a further 30 minutes or until golden. Set aside for 10 minutes to stand before serving.

Nutrition Information

- Calories: 401.52 calories
- Total Carbohydrate: 37 grams carbohydrates
- Protein: 9 grams protein
- Total Fat: 25 grams fat
- Saturated Fat: 14 grams saturated fat

42. Layered Potato Cake

Serving: 4 | Prep: 20mins | Ready in: 80mins

Ingredients

- Melted butter, to grease
- 6 (about 1kg) coliban potatoes, peeled, thinly sliced
- 70g butter, melted
- 30g (1/3 cup) shredded parmesan or vegetarian hard cheese
- 1 teaspoon fresh thyme leaves
- Salt freshly ground black pepper
- Mixed salad leaves, to serve

Direction

- Preheat oven to 220C. Brush a round 18cm (base measurement) cake pan with melted butter to lightly grease. Place the potato slices in a large bowl. Add the melted butter and gently toss until potato slices are well coated.

Arrange one-third of the potato slices over the base of the prepared pan.
- Combine parmesan and thyme in a bowl. Sprinkle potato slices with one-third of the parmesan mixture. Season with salt and pepper. Continue layering with the remaining potato slices, parmesan mixture and salt and pepper, finishing with a layer of parmesan mixture.
- Bake in preheated oven, pressing the potato down with the back of a large spoon a couple of times during cooking, for 1 hour or until tender and golden. Remove from oven and set aside for 5 minutes to cool slightly. Turn onto a serving plate. Cut into wedges and serve with mixed salad leaves.

Nutrition Information

- Calories: 314.046 calories
- Protein: 9 grams protein
- Sodium: 215.09 milligrams sodium
- Total Fat: 16 grams fat
- Saturated Fat: 11 grams saturated fat
- Total Carbohydrate: 31 grams carbohydrates
- Sugar: 2 grams sugar

43. Louise's Two Potato Gratin

Serving: 6 | Prep: 25mins | Ready in: 95mins

Ingredients

- 1 tablespoon extra virgin olive oil
- 1 brown onion, finely chopped
- 1 garlic clove, finely chopped
- 375ml (1 1/2 cups) milk
- 160ml (2/3 cup) chicken stock, or vegetable stock
- 2-3 sprigs fresh lemon thyme or thyme
- 900g Carisma potatoes, or Nicola potatoes, unpeeled, scrubbed
- 650g sweet potato, peeled
- 50g (2/3 cup) finely grated parmesan
- Fresh thyme sprigs, to serve (optional)

Direction

- Heat the oil in a frying pan over medium-low heat. Add the onion and garlic. Cook, stirring often, for 4-5 minutes until the onion is soft and golden but not browned. Add the milk, stock and thyme. Gently heat the mixture over a low heat until almost boiling (do not boil or the mixture will curdle). Season with pepper and set aside.
- Preheat oven to 180C/160C fan forced. Grease a 6.5cm-deep, 19.5 x 29.5cm (base measurement) ovenproof baking dish. Use a mandolin or sharp knife to thinly slice the potatoes and sweet potato. Layer half of the potato and sweet potato slices in the prepared dish, slightly overlapping, pressing down firmly as you go. Sprinkle over half the parmesan. Ladle over half the warm milk mixture. Layer over the remaining potato and sweet potato and ladle over the remaining milk mixture. Sprinkle over the remaining parmesan. Set aside for 5 minutes to soak.
- Cover the dish with foil. Bake for 50 minutes. Increase the oven to 200C/180C. Uncover the dish and bake for a further 20-25 minutes or until the potato is soft and tender and the top is golden and crunchy. Sprinkle with the extra thyme, if using.

Nutrition Information

- Calories: 301.857 calories
- Total Fat: 8 grams fat
- Saturated Fat: 3 grams saturated fat
- Total Carbohydrate: 43 grams carbohydrates
- Protein: 12 grams protein

44. Low Fat Creamy Potato Gratin With Parmesan Crumbs

Serving: 6 | Prep: 20mins | Ready in: 125mins

Ingredients

- Olive oil spray
- 1kg Lady Christl potatoes, peeled, thinly sliced (see note)
- 1/2 garlic clove, finely chopped
- 250ml (1 cup) Massel chicken style liquid stock
- 200ml light thickened cooking cream
- 35g (1/2 cup) fresh breadcrumbs
- 1 tablespoon shredded parmesan

Direction

- Preheat oven to 160°C. Spray a 1.25L (5-cup) capacity baking dish with oil. Arrange a layer of potato, overlapping slightly, over the base. Sprinkle with a little of the garlic. Season with salt and pepper. Continue layering with remaining potato and garlic.
- Combine the stock and cream in a jug. Pour the cream mixture over the potato. Bake for 1 hour 15 minutes.
- Combine breadcrumbs and parmesan. Sprinkle evenly over the potato. Bake for a further 30 minutes or until golden. Set aside for 5 minutes to cool slightly.

Nutrition Information

- Calories: 195.98 calories
- Total Fat: 7.5 grams fat
- Saturated Fat: 4.5 grams saturated fat
- Total Carbohydrate: 25 grams carbohydrates
- Protein: 6.5 grams protein

45. Mashed Potato And Bacon Bake

Serving: 6 | Prep: 25mins | Ready in: 80mins

Ingredients

- 2kg sebago potatoes, peeled, roughly chopped
- 2 garlic cloves, peeled
- 80g butter, softened
- 200g middle bacon rashers, trimmed, chopped
- 250g cream cheese, chopped, softened
- 1/2 cup milk
- 3 green onions, thinly sliced, plus extra, sliced, to serve
- 1/2 cup grated perfect bakes cheese mix

Direction

- Preheat oven to 200C/180C fan-forced. Grease a 5cm-deep, 25cm round baking dish.
- Place potato and garlic in a large saucepan. Cover with cold water. Bring to the boil over high heat. Reduce heat to medium. Simmer for 15 minutes or until tender. Drain. Return potato and garlic to pan. Toss over low heat for 1 to 2 minutes or until excess water has evaporated.
- Meanwhile, melt 20g butter in a frying pan over medium-high heat. Add bacon. Cook, stirring occasionally, for 5 minutes or until golden. Drain on paper towel.
- Using a potato masher, mash potato until smooth. Add cream cheese and remaining butter. Using a wooden spoon, beat until smooth and combined. Gradually stir in milk. Stir in onion and half the bacon. Season with salt and pepper.
- Spoon mash into prepared baking dish. Sprinkle with cheese and remaining bacon. Bake for 30 minutes or until golden. Stand for 5 minutes. Serve sprinkled with extra onion.

Nutrition Information

- Calories: 573.361 calories
- Saturated Fat: 22.1 grams saturated fat
- Total Carbohydrate: 41.7 grams carbohydrates
- Protein: 21.8 grams protein
- Cholesterol: 101 milligrams cholesterol
- Sodium: 858 milligrams sodium
- Total Fat: 33.5 grams fat

46. Moroccan Sweet Potato Bake

Serving: 4 | Prep: 10mins | Ready in: 70mins

Ingredients

- 1 tablespoon Moroccan seasoning
- 2 teaspoons mild paprika
- 1/4 teaspoon dried chilli flakes
- 1/4 cup roughly chopped fresh coriander leaves
- 1kg small orange sweet potatoes, cut into thick wedges
- 1 bunch Dutch (baby) carrots, trimmed, scrubbed
- 1/3 cup extra virgin olive oil
- 1 red onion, halved, cut into wedges
- 1 red capsicum, slickly sliced
- 1 cup wholemeal couscous
- 3/4 cup plain Greek-style yoghurt
- 2 teaspoons finely grated lemon rind
- 1 tablespoon lemon juice
- Fresh coriander sprigs, to serve
- Lemon wedges, to serve

Direction

- Preheat oven to 200C/180C fan-forced. Line 2 large baking trays with baking paper.
- Combine seasoning, paprika, chilli and coriander in a small bowl. Place sweet potato and carrots in a large bowl. Drizzle vegetables with 2 1/2 tablespoons oil and sprinkle with 3/4 of the spice mix. Rub to coat. Place, in a single layer, on prepared trays. Bake for 20 minutes.
- Place onion and capsicum in bowl. Drizzle with 1 tablespoon oil. Sprinkle with remaining spice mix. Rub to coat. Add to potato and carrot in oven. Bake for a further 25 minutes or until vegetables are golden and tender.
- Meanwhile, place couscous in a 4.5cm deep, 26cm round (4-cup-capacity) baking dish. Pour over 1 cup cold water and drizzle with remaining oil. Season with salt and pepper. Cover with foil. Bake for 15 minutes or until liquid is absorbed. Remove and discard foil. Fluff with a fork to separate grains.
- Combine yoghurt, lemon rind and lemon juice in a small bowl. Spoon vegetables on top of couscous. Drizzle with yoghurt mixture. Top with coriander sprigs and serve with lemon wedges.

Nutrition Information

- Calories: 615.425 calories
- Total Carbohydrate: 73.3 grams carbohydrates
- Cholesterol: 9 milligrams cholesterol
- Sodium: 784 milligrams sodium
- Saturated Fat: 5.9 grams saturated fat
- Total Fat: 25.6 grams fat
- Protein: 16.1 grams protein

47. Mustard Balsamic Beef With Creamy Potato Bake

Serving: 4 | Prep: 20mins | Ready in: 80mins

Ingredients

- 1 tablespoon wholegrain mustard
- 1 tablespoon white balsamic vinegar
- 1 tablespoon olive oil
- 4 x 125g beef sirloin steaks
- 1kg sebago potatoes, peeled, thinly sliced
- 1 small brown onion, halved, thinly sliced
- 1 cup Kraft pizza 4 cheese blend
- 2.3 cup pure cream
- Mixed salad leaves, to serve

Direction

- Combine mustard, vinegar and oil in a glass or ceramic dish. Add steak. Turn to coat. Cover. Refrigerate for 2 hours or overnight, if time permits.
- Preheat oven to 180°C/160°C fan-forced. Grease a 6cm deep, 24cm (base) square baking dish.

- Arrange 1/3 of potato, overlapping slightly, over base of dish. Sprinkle with half the onion and 1/3 of cheese. Repeat layers. Arrange remaining potato over top and sprinkle with remaining cheese. Pour over cream. Bake for 1 hour or until potato is tender and top is golden.
- Meanwhile, heat a chargrill pan over high heat. Reduce heat to medium-high. Cook steaks for 3 to 4 minutes each side for medium, or until cooked to your liking. Transfer to a plate. Cover with foil. Rest for 5 minutes. Thickly slice steaks. Serve with creamy potato bake and salad leaves.

Nutrition Information

- Calories: 954.805 calories
- Protein: 48 grams protein
- Cholesterol: 241 milligrams cholesterol
- Total Fat: 69 grams fat
- Total Carbohydrate: 35 grams carbohydrates
- Sugar: 6 grams sugar
- Saturated Fat: 41 grams saturated fat
- Sodium: 424.67 milligrams sodium

48. Parmesan, Potato Leek Bake

Serving: 6 | Prep: 10mins | Ready in: 70mins

Ingredients

- 35g (1/3 cup) coarsely grated vintage cheddar
- 30g (1/3 cup) finely shredded parmesan
- 2 tablespoons finely chopped fresh thyme
- 2 tablespoons finely chopped fresh oregano
- 4 large (about 800g) desiree potatoes, unpeeled, thinly sliced
- 1 leek, halved lengthways, washed, thinly sliced crossways
- 300ml thickened cream
- 125ml (1/2 cup) dry white wine
- 1 garlic clove, crushed
- Salt freshly ground black pepper
- Pinch of mild paprika

Direction

- Preheat oven to 180°C. Combine the cheddar and parmesan in a bowl. Combine the thyme and oregano in a separate bowl.
- Arrange half the potato and leek slices over the base of a square 19cm (base measurement), 1.5L (6-cup) capacity ovenproof dish. Top with half the cheese mixture and half the thyme mixture. Repeat with remaining potato, leek and cheese mixture.
- Combine cream, wine and garlic in a jug. Season with salt and pepper. Pour over potato mixture. Sprinkle with paprika and cover with foil. Bake in oven for 45 minutes. Uncover and cook for 15 minutes or until brown and tender. Remove from oven and sprinkle with remaining thyme mixture. Serve immediately.

Nutrition Information

- Calories: 314.763 calories
- Saturated Fat: 14 grams saturated fat
- Sodium: 146.68 milligrams sodium
- Protein: 8 grams protein
- Cholesterol: 61 milligrams cholesterol
- Total Fat: 22 grams fat
- Total Carbohydrate: 17 grams carbohydrates
- Sugar: 4 grams sugar

49. Parsnip, Leek And Potato Gratin With Pecan Crumble

Serving: 8 | Prep: 30mins | Ready in: 95mins

Ingredients

- 1 large parsnip, peeled, very thinly sliced into rounds
- 1 leek, trimmed, halved, sliced
- 1kg sebago potatoes, peeled, very thinly sliced
- 1 cup pure cream

- 1 cup milk
- 1 garlic clove, crushed
- 2 teaspoons chopped fresh thyme leaves
- 3/4 cup finely grated parmesan
- 1/2 cup pecans, roughly chopped
- 1/3 cup panko breadcrumbs
- 1 tablespoon extra virgin olive oil
- Fresh flat-leaf parsley leaves, to serve

Direction

- Preheat oven to 180C/160C fan-forced.
- Toss parsnip, leek and potato in a bowl. Layer vegetables in a 6cm-deep, 20cm x 30cm ovenproof dish.
- Whisk cream, milk, garlic, thyme and parmesan in a jug. Season with salt and pepper. Pour over vegetables in dish. Bake for 30 minutes.
- Place pecans and breadcrumbs in a bowl. Season with salt and pepper. Sprinkle over top of gratin. Drizzle with oil. Bake for a further 20 minutes or until breadcrumbs are golden. Cover loosely with foil. Bake for 15 minutes or until vegetables are tender. Stand for 10 minutes. Sprinkle with parsley. Serve.

Nutrition Information

- Calories: 357.066 calories
- Total Carbohydrate: 23.4 grams carbohydrates
- Protein: 9.6 grams protein
- Cholesterol: 42 milligrams cholesterol
- Sodium: 225 milligrams sodium
- Total Fat: 24.1 grams fat
- Saturated Fat: 11 grams saturated fat

50. Pommes Anna

Serving: 8 | Prep: 30mins | Ready in: 90mins

Ingredients

- 1kg sebago potatoes, peeled
- 1/4 cup olive oil
- 1/4 teaspoon ground nutmeg
- 60g butter, chopped

Direction

- Using a mandoline slicer, slice potatoes into very thin rounds. Place in a large bowl and drizzle with oil. Season with salt, pepper and a pinch nutmeg. Toss potato in oil mixture to coat.
- Preheat oven to 180C. Cut eight strips of baking paper. Use paper to line eight 3/4-cup capacity Texas muffin pan holes. Divide potato between muffin holes, pressing in to compact potato. Top with butter. Sprinkle with a little of remaining nutmeg. Bake for 1 hour or until crisp and golden.
- Loosen potato using flat-bladed knife. Use paper to lift out onto plates. Serve.

Nutrition Information

- Calories: 195.98 calories
- Sugar: 1 grams sugar
- Total Carbohydrate: 15 grams carbohydrates
- Total Fat: 13 grams fat
- Saturated Fat: 5 grams saturated fat
- Protein: 3 grams protein
- Sodium: 51.15 milligrams sodium

51. Potato Onion Gratin

Serving: 6 | Prep: 40mins | Ready in: 105mins

Ingredients

- Melted butter, to grease
- 250ml (1 cup) pouring cream
- 125ml (1/2 cup) milk
- 1 small brown onion, thinly sliced into rings
- 1kg brushed potatoes, peeled, thinly sliced
- 80g (1 cup) coarsely grated cheddar

Direction

- Preheat oven to 180°C. Brush a 1.75L (7-cup) capacity baking dish with melted butter. Place the cream, milk and onion in a saucepan over medium heat. Cook for 3-4 minutes or until almost boiling. Remove from heat. Season with salt and pepper. Set aside for 10 minutes to cool slightly. Transfer onion to a plate.
- Place one-third of the potato, overlapping, in the base of dish. Top with one-third of the onion and one-third of the cheddar. Repeat with remaining potato, onion and cheddar.
- Pour over cream mixture. Place dish on a baking tray. Bake for 1 hour or until potato is tender and top is crisp and golden. Set aside for 10 minutes to cool slightly before serving.

Nutrition Information

- Calories: 334.6 calories
- Protein: 8.5 grams protein
- Total Fat: 24 grams fat
- Total Carbohydrate: 22 grams carbohydrates
- Saturated Fat: 15 grams saturated fat

52. Potato Parsnip Gratin

Serving: 6 | Prep: 15mins | Ready in: 75mins

Ingredients

- Melted butter, to grease
- 650g potatoes, peeled, cut crossways into 2mm-thick slices
- 650g parsnips, peeled, cut crossways into 2mm-thick slices
- 1 large brown onion, halved, thinly sliced
- 2 tablespoons chopped fresh rosemary
- 500ml (2 cups) Massel chicken style liquid stock
- 250ml (1 cup) milk
- 25g butter, finely chopped

Direction

- Preheat oven to 190°C. Brush a 2L (8-cup) capacity ovenproof dish with melted butter to lightly grease. Place the potato, parsnip, onion and rosemary in a large bowl and toss to combine. Season with salt and pepper.
- Spread the potato mixture over the base of the prepared dish. Pour over the stock and milk. Top with the butter. Bake in oven for 1 hour or until golden and the vegetables are tender when tested with a skewer. Set aside for 5 minutes to stand. Serve.

Nutrition Information

- Calories: 206.735 calories
- Total Fat: 6.5 grams fat
- Saturated Fat: 4 grams saturated fat
- Total Carbohydrate: 30 grams carbohydrates
- Protein: 7.5 grams protein

53. Potato And Beef Ragu Lasagne

Serving: 8 | Prep: 60mins | Ready in: 260mins

Ingredients

- 2 tablespoons vegetable oil
- 2 brown onions, finely chopped
- 3 garlic cloves, chopped
- 1kg beef chuck steak, trimmed, cut into 3cm pieces
- 1L (4 cups) Massel beef stock
- 690g btl Val Verde Traditional Pasta Sauce
- 250ml (1 cup) red wine
- 4 fresh thyme sprigs
- 60g baby spinach leaves
- 100g butter
- 75g (1/2 cup) plain flour
- 1L (4 cups) milk
- 20g (1/4 cup) finely grated parmesan
- 40g (1/3 cup) coarsely grated fresh mozzarella

- 4 (about 780g) large Red Delight potatoes, thinly sliced

Direction

- Heat the oil in a large, heavy-based saucepan over medium-high heat. Add the onion and garlic. Stir for 3 minutes or until soft. Stir in beef, stock, pasta sauce, red wine and thyme. Bring to boil. Reduce heat to low and simmer, stirring occasionally, for 2 hours or until beef is tender and mixture thickens. Add the spinach. Stir for 2 minutes or until spinach just wilts. Season with pepper. Discard thyme stems.
- Melt the butter in a saucepan over medium-high heat until foaming. Add flour and cook, stirring, for 2 minutes or until the mixture bubbles. Remove from heat. Gradually add the milk, stirring, until smooth. Cook over medium-high heat, stirring, for 3 minutes or until the sauce thickens. Cook, whisking, for 1 minute. Remove from heat. Stir in the parmesan and mozzarella. Season.
- Preheat oven to 180C. Place potato in a microwave-safe bowl. Cover and cook in a microwave on high for 5-6 minutes or until just tender. Refresh under cold water. Drain. Place one-third of potato, in a single layer, in a 4L (16-cup) baking dish. Top with half the beef mixture. Continue layering with remaining potato and beef mixture, finishing with potato. Top with white sauce. Bake on a baking tray for 1 hour or until golden. Cool for 15 minutes.

Nutrition Information

- Calories: 579.575 calories
- Total Carbohydrate: 40 grams carbohydrates
- Protein: 37 grams protein
- Total Fat: 28 grams fat
- Saturated Fat: 14 grams saturated fat

54. Potato And Celeriac Bake

Serving: 8 | Prep: 40mins | Ready in: 135mins

Ingredients

- 3 teaspoons olive oil
- 1 brown onion, finely chopped
- 600ml milk
- 150ml Massel chicken style liquid stock
- 45g butter, chopped
- 40g (1/4 cup) flour
- 250g mozzarella, coarsely grated
- 750g potatoes, peeled, very thinly sliced
- 750g celeriac, peeled, very thinly sliced
- 500g smoked ham, chopped
- 200g finely grated parmesan
- Fresh continental parsley leaves, to serve

Direction

- Preheat oven to 180C/160C fan forced. Lightly grease a 6.5cm-deep, 20 x 30cm baking dish.
- Heat the oil in a frying pan over medium heat. Add the onion and cook, stirring occasionally, for 8-10 minutes or until lightly golden and caramelised.
- Meanwhile, heat the milk and stock in a saucepan over low heat until the mixture almost comes to the boil. Remove from the heat. Melt the butter in a separate saucepan over low heat. Add the flour and cook, stirring, for 1-2 minutes or until smooth. Remove from heat and slowly add the warm milk mixture, whisking constantly until smooth. Stir over low heat for 5 minutes or until the sauce thickens slightly.
- Add mozzarella and onion to the béchamel. Stir until cheese is mostly melted. Season with pepper.
- Arrange a layer of potato and then celeriac slices over the base of the prepared dish. Sprinkle with one-third of the ham. Spread with one-third of the béchamel sauce. Repeat the layering 2 more times with the potato, celeriac, ham and béchamel sauce. Cover with

foil and bake for 1 hour 15 minutes or until potato and celeriac are tender.
- Uncover and sprinkle evenly with the parmesan. Bake for a further 10 minutes or until the parmesan is melted and golden. Set aside for 10 minutes before serving. Sprinkle with parsley leaves.

Nutrition Information

- Calories: 505.963 calories
- Total Carbohydrate: 23 grams carbohydrates
- Protein: 35 grams protein
- Total Fat: 28 grams fat
- Saturated Fat: 16 grams saturated fat

55. Potato And Fennel 'bake' Recipe

Serving: 4 | Prep: 20mins | Ready in: 250mins

Ingredients

- 1 small fennel bulb
- 1 leek, trimmed, thinly sliced
- 2 large garlic cloves, very finely chopped
- 1kg coliban potatoes, very thinly sliced
- 100g (1 cup) pre-grated 3 cheese blend
- 300ml ctn cooking cream
- 40g (1/2 cup) finely grated parmesan
- 1 small red onion, thinly sliced into rounds
- 1/4 cup small fresh parsley leaves

Direction

- Trim the fronds from the fennel and reserve. Thinly slice the fennel and transfer to a bowl. Add the leek and garlic. Toss to combine.
- Lightly grease the bowl of a 5.5L slow cooker and line with baking paper. Arrange one-third of the potato, overlapping slightly, in the base of the prepared slow cooker. Sprinkle with one-third of the fennel mixture and one-third of the cheese blend. Drizzle with one-third of the cream. Season.
- Repeat layering the remaining potato, fennel mixture, cheese blend and cream. Cover and cook on High for 3 hours 30 minutes or until the potato is tender. Sprinkle with the parmesan, cover and cook for a further 20 minutes or until cheese has melted.
- Repeat layering the remaining potato, fennel mixture, cheese blend and cream. Cover and cook on High for 3 hours 30 minutes or until the potato is tender. Sprinkle with the parmesan, cover and cook for a further 20 minutes or until cheese has melted.

Nutrition Information

- Calories: 563.801 calories
- Protein: 19.5 grams protein
- Total Carbohydrate: 35.8 grams carbohydrates
- Total Fat: 36.6 grams fat
- Saturated Fat: 23.2 grams saturated fat

56. Potato And Leek Gratin

Serving: 4 | Prep: 30mins | Ready in: 100mins

Ingredients

- 4 slices prosciutto, chopped
- 2 medium leeks, trimmed, halved washed, sliced
- 400g desiree potatoes, thinly sliced
- 1/2 cup grated tasty cheese
- Fresh flat-leaf parsley leaves, to serve
- 1/4 cup milk
- 1/4 cup pure cream
- 2 garlic cloves, crushed

Direction

- Preheat oven to 180°C/160°C fan-forced. Lightly grease a 6 cup-capacity baking dish.

- Make milk mixture: Combine milk, cream and garlic in a jug. Season with salt and pepper.
- Heat a non-stick frying pan over medium-high heat. Add prosciutto and leek. Cook for 5 to 6 minutes or until leek is tender.
- Layer one-quarter potato over base of prepared dish. Top with one-third leek mixture. Repeat layers, finishing with potato.
- Pour milk mixture over potato mixture. Sprinkle with cheese. Bake for 45 to 50 minutes or until potato is tender and cheese golden. Stand for 5 minutes. Serve.

Nutrition Information

- Calories: 263.617 calories
- Total Fat: 15.2 grams fat
- Protein: 13 grams protein
- Cholesterol: 53 milligrams cholesterol
- Saturated Fat: 9.3 grams saturated fat
- Total Carbohydrate: 16.7 grams carbohydrates
- Sodium: 583 milligrams sodium

57. Potato Gratins

Serving: 8 | Prep: 20mins | Ready in: 95mins

Ingredients

- Butter, at room temperature, to grease
- 1.5kg potatoes, peeled, thinly sliced
- 750ml (3 cups) milk
- 250ml (1 cup) thickened cream
- 2 fresh thyme sprigs, bruised
- Pinch of ground nutmeg
- 1 brown onion, halved, thinly sliced
- 30g (1/3 cup) finely grated parmesan

Direction

- Brush a 23 x 30cm (2L) capacity baking dish with butter to lightly grease.
- Place the potato, milk, cream, thyme and nutmeg in a large saucepan. Season with salt and pepper. Bring to the boil slowly over medium heat. Reduce heat to medium-low and simmer gently for 5 minutes or until the potato is slightly tender.
- Arrange half the potato mixture over the base of the prepared dish. Top with the onion. Spread the remaining potato mixture over the top and press down slightly. Cover with foil. Bake in oven for 30 minutes. Uncover and bake for a further 15-20 minutes or until golden. Set aside for 2 hours to cool completely. Cover and place in the fridge overnight to chill.
- Preheat oven to 200°C. Line a baking tray with non-stick baking paper. Cut the potato gratin into 8 portions. Transfer to the lined tray.
- Sprinkle with the parmesan. Bake in oven for 15-20 minutes or until heated through. Serve.

Nutrition Information

- Calories: 302.335 calories
- Total Fat: 17 grams fat
- Saturated Fat: 11 grams saturated fat
- Total Carbohydrate: 28 grams carbohydrates
- Protein: 9.5 grams protein

58. Potato Tortilla

Serving: 8 | Prep: 20mins | Ready in: 70mins

Ingredients

- 60ml (1/4 cup) olive oil
- 200g speck, cut into 1cm pieces
- 1 brown onion, halved, thinly sliced
- 4 garlic cloves, crushed
- 3 (about 600g) desiree potatoes, peeled, thinly sliced
- 8 eggs
- Salt freshly ground black pepper

Direction

- Heat 1 tablespoon of the oil in a 30cm (base measurement) frying pan over medium-high heat. Add the speck, onion and garlic and cook, stirring, for 10 minutes or until onion softens. Transfer to a bowl.
- Heat the remaining oil in the same pan. Add the potato and cook, stirring occasionally, for 25 minutes or until golden brown and tender.
- Preheat grill on high. Place eggs in a bowl and whisk until combined. Season with salt and pepper.
- Sprinkle potato with onion mixture. Pour egg over the potato mixture, shaking gently to loosen from the base of the pan. Cook over medium-high heat for 8 minutes or until the base of the tortilla is golden and set.
- Place tortilla under preheated grill, about 6cm from heat source, and cook for 5 minutes or until golden and set.
- Use a round-bladed knife to loosen edges of tortilla. Set aside for 5 minutes to cool. Cut into wedges to serve.

Nutrition Information

- Calories: 255.013 calories
- Saturated Fat: 5 grams saturated fat
- Protein: 13 grams protein
- Total Fat: 18 grams fat
- Total Carbohydrate: 10 grams carbohydrates
- Sugar: 1 grams sugar
- Sodium: 523.63 milligrams sodium

59. Potato, Bacon Blue Cheese Bake

Serving: 6 | Prep: 10mins | Ready in: 90mins

Ingredients

- 1 250g pkt rindless short cut bacon
- 1kg desiree potatoes, unpeeled, quartered
- 2 red onions, halved, each half cut into 3 wedges
- 80g piece blue cheese (King Island Dairy brand), chopped
- Salt freshly ground black pepper
- 1 tablespoon fresh thyme leaves
- 160ml (2/3 cup) thickened cream
- 160ml (2/3 cup) Massel chicken style liquid stock

Direction

- Preheat oven to 190°C. Use a sharp knife to cut each bacon rasher, crossways, into 1cm-thick slices.
- Combine the potatoes, onions, bacon and half the blue cheese in a large bowl. Season with salt and pepper. Spoon into a rectangular or square 2.5L (10-cup capacity) ovenproof baking dish. Sprinkle over the thyme leaves.
- Use a fork to whisk together cream and chicken stock in a jug, and pour over the potatoes. Sprinkle with remaining blue cheese. Cook, uncovered, in preheated oven for 1 hour 20 minutes or until golden brown. Serve immediately.

Nutrition Information

- Calories: 333.405 calories
- Total Fat: 20 grams fat
- Saturated Fat: 11 grams saturated fat
- Sodium: 851.11 milligrams sodium
- Sugar: 5 grams sugar
- Protein: 16 grams protein
- Cholesterol: 66 milligrams cholesterol
- Total Carbohydrate: 21 grams carbohydrates

60. Potato, Bacon And Leek Gratin

Serving: 4 | Prep: 15mins | Ready in: 40mins

Ingredients

- 1kg chat potatoes, quartered

- 4 rashers middle bacon, rind removed, trimmed, chopped
- 1 medium leek, trimmed, halved, washed, thinly sliced
- 1 garlic clove, crushed
- 1 cup reduced-fat sour cream
- 1 cup grated reduced-fat tasty cheese

Direction

- Preheat oven to 180°C/160°C fan-forced. Place potato in a saucepan of boiling, salted water over high heat. Cook for 10 to 12 minutes or until just tender. Drain.
- Grease a 7cm-deep, 8 cup-capacity ovenproof dish. Combine potato, bacon, leek, garlic, sour cream and half the cheese in a bowl. Season with pepper. Transfer to prepared dish. Sprinkle over remaining cheese. Bake for 25 minutes or until potato is tender and cheese melted and golden. Serve.

Nutrition Information

- Calories: 474.176 calories
- Total Carbohydrate: 37 grams carbohydrates
- Total Fat: 22.6 grams fat
- Saturated Fat: 13.5 grams saturated fat
- Protein: 26.7 grams protein
- Cholesterol: 84 milligrams cholesterol
- Sodium: 888 milligrams sodium

61. Potato, Blue Cheese And Pine Nut Bake

Serving: 4 | Prep: 20mins | Ready in: 75mins

Ingredients

- olive oil cooking spray
- 2 (500g) desiree potatoes, peeled, thinly sliced
- 350g butternut pumpkin, peeled, thinly sliced
- 1 large brown onion, peeled, thinly sliced
- 1 cup Massel chicken style liquid stock
- 2 teaspoons pureed garlic
- 60g mild blue cheese, finely chopped
- 60g reduced-fat ricotta cheese
- 1/3 cup pine nuts
- 1/4 cup chopped fresh flat-leaf parsley leaves

Direction

- Preheat oven to 200°C. Lightly spray a 6cm-deep, 11cm x 21cm (base) loaf pan with cooking spray.
- Layer potato, pumpkin and onion in prepared pan. Combine stock and pureed garlic in a bowl. Pour over vegetable layers. Cover with foil. Bake for 45 minutes or until vegetables are tender. Remove from oven.
- Meanwhile, combine blue cheese, ricotta and pine nuts in a bowl. Spoon over vegetables. Season with pepper. Bake for a further 10 minutes or until golden.
- Sprinkle with parsley. Serve.

Nutrition Information

- Calories: 309.983 calories
- Total Fat: 17 grams fat
- Saturated Fat: 4 grams saturated fat
- Total Carbohydrate: 25 grams carbohydrates
- Sugar: 9 grams sugar
- Protein: 12 grams protein
- Sodium: 465.18 milligrams sodium

62. Prosciutto Stuffed Potato Bake

Serving: 10 | Prep: 30mins | Ready in: 180mins

Ingredients

- 450ml pouring cream
- 185ml (3/4 cup) milk
- 2kg potatoes, peeled, thinly sliced lengthways
- 1 small brown onion, halved, thinly sliced
- 100g prosciutto, halved lengthways
- 20g (1/4 cup) finely grated parmesan

Direction

- Preheat the oven to 170C/150C fan forced. Combine the cream and milk in a jug. Season well.
- Stand the potato slices upright in rows across the base of a 6cm-deep, 4L round ovenproof baking dish. Arrange the onion slices between the potato slices. Pour over the cream mixture.
- Cover the dish with foil and place on a baking tray. Bake for 1 1/2 hours or until the potato is tender.
- Increase the oven temperature to 180C/160C fan forced. Remove the foil from the potato bake and carefully weave the prosciutto between some of the potato slices. Sprinkle with parmesan. Return to the oven and bake, uncovered, for 1 hour or until golden brown and the potato is very tender.

63. Provencal Potato Bake

Serving: 6 | Prep: 5mins | Ready in: 75mins

Ingredients

- 1kg chat potatoes
- 1/2 cup (100g) salted capers, rinsed, drained
- 1 cup (120g) pitted black olives
- 1 tablespoon thyme leaves
- 4 rosemary sprigs, broken into small pieces
- 1/2 cup (125ml) extra virgin olive oil
- 2 tablespoons white wine vinegar
- 1 tablespoon finely chopped flat-leaf parsley

Direction

- Preheat the oven to 220°C and line a baking tray with baking paper.
- Place the potatoes in a pan and cover with cold, salted water. Bring to the boil over medium-high heat, then reduce heat to medium and simmer for 10-12 minutes until just tender. Drain well and set aside to cool slightly.
- Crush the potatoes very lightly with a fork, then place in a bowl with the capers, olives, thyme and rosemary, then season. Add 1/3 cup (80ml) oil and toss well to coat the potatoes. Tip onto the baking tray. Whisk the vinegar and remaining 2 tablespoons oil together, then drizzle over the potatoes.
- Bake for 45 minutes or until golden and crisp. Scatter with parsley and serve.

Nutrition Information

- Calories: 316.436 calories
- Total Fat: 23 grams fat
- Sugar: 3 grams sugar
- Sodium: 277.97 milligrams sodium
- Saturated Fat: 4 grams saturated fat
- Total Carbohydrate: 23 grams carbohydrates
- Protein: 4 grams protein

64. Quick Chicken And Garlic Potato 'bake'

Serving: 4 | Prep: 15mins | Ready in: 45mins

Ingredients

- 60g butter
- 2 leeks, washed, thinly sliced (see note)
- 5 garlic cloves, crushed
- 2 tablespoons plain flour
- 1 1/3 cups milk
- 4 (580g) chicken thigh fillets, trimmed, cut into 1.5cm cubes
- 3/4 cup grated cheddar
- 1/2 x 800g pkt McCain Roast Potatoes (Rosemary and Garlic)
- Mixed green salad, to serve (see note)

Direction

- Preheat oven to 220C or 200C fan-forced. Place a baking tray in oven.

- Place potatoes on hot tray. Roast for 15 minutes.
- Meanwhile, melt butter in a large saucepan over medium heat. Cook leek, stirring for 5 minutes. Cover and cook for another 5 minutes or until softened. Stir through garlic and cook for 1 minute. Stir in flour and cook for 30 seconds. Add milk and stir until combined. Add chicken and bring to a simmer. Cook, covered, for 5 minutes or until chicken is just cooked. Remove from heat and stir through cheese. Season.
- Transfer to a 5 cup ovenproof baking dish. Arrange sliced potato on top. Spray with oil. Cook under grill, 15cm from heat source for 15 minutes or until top is golden and crunchy. Serve with a mixed green salad.

65. Quick Creamy Chicken And Sweet Potato Bake

Serving: 6 | Prep: 20mins | Ready in: 65mins

Ingredients

- 1.1kg sweet potatoes, peeled, cut into 5mm-slices
- 300ml Bulla Creme Fraiche
- 125ml (1/2 cup) Bulla Cooking Cream
- 2 garlic cloves, crushed
- 1 tablespoon chopped fresh tarragon
- 200g meat from barbecue chicken, shredded
- 2 green shallots, chopped
- 105g (1 1/4 cups) grated cheddar cheese

Direction

- Preheat oven to 200C/180C fan forced. Place the sweet potato in a large microwave-safe bowl with 60ml (1/4 cup) water. Cover with two sheets of plastic wrap. Cook in the microwave on High for 8 minutes or until tender. Drain and set aside.
- Meanwhile, lightly grease a 6cm-high 30 x 20cm (base measurement) baking dish. Combine the crème fraiche, cooking cream, garlic and tarragon in a jug. Season.
- Layer the sweet potato, chicken, shallot and 80g (1 cup) of the cheese in the prepared dish, pouring a little of the cream mixture between each layer. Pour the remaining cream mixture over the top. Scatter over the remaining cheese and bake for 30-35 minutes or until golden and the cheese is melted and bubbling. Set aside for 10 minutes before serving.

66. Reduced Fat Chicken And Leek Potato Bake

Serving: 4 | Prep: 15mins | Ready in: 80mins

Ingredients

- Olive oil cooking spray
- 1 large (280g) chicken breast fillet, trimmed, thinly sliced
- 3 garlic cloves, crushed
- 1 tablespoon fresh thyme leaves
- 1 leek, trimmed, halved, washed, sliced
- 800g desiree potatoes, thinly sliced
- 1 cup reduced-fat grated tasty cheese
- 300ml light cooking cream

Direction

- Preheat oven to 180°C/160°C fan-forced. Grease a 7cm-deep, 19.5cm (base) square baking dish.
- Spray a non-stick frying pan with oil. Heat over medium-high heat. Add chicken. Cook, stirring, for 4 to 5 minutes or until cooked through. Transfer to a plate. Add garlic, thyme and leek to pan. Cook for 4 to 5 minutes or until softened.
- Layer one-third potato over base of prepared dish. Top with half the chicken and leek mixture. Sprinkle with one-third cheese. Drizzle with one-third cream. Repeat layers, ending with potato. Add remaining cream. Sprinkle with remaining cheese. Cover with

foil. Bake for 50 minutes or until potato is tender. Remove cover.
- Increase oven to 200°C/180°C fan-forced. Bake for 10 to 15 minutes or until golden. Stand for 10 minutes. Serve.

Nutrition Information

- Calories: 438.804 calories
- Cholesterol: 101 milligrams cholesterol
- Saturated Fat: 14 grams saturated fat
- Total Carbohydrate: 26 grams carbohydrates
- Sugar: 7 grams sugar
- Total Fat: 22 grams fat
- Protein: 32 grams protein
- Sodium: 227.82 milligrams sodium

67. Scalloped Potatoes

Serving: 4 | Prep: 30mins | Ready in: 95mins

Ingredients

- 20g salted butter
- 1 onion, halved, thinly sliced
- 1kg Desiree potatoes
- 300ml carton pouring cream (see variation)
- pinch of Ground Nutmeg

Direction

- Preheat oven to 200C/180C fan-forced. Lightly grease a 6cm deep, 15cm x 24cm (base) ovenproof dish.
- Melt butter in a frying pan over medium heat. Add onion. Cook for 4 minutes or until soft. Remove from heat. Set aside. Slice potatoes into 5mm-thick rounds. Pour cream into a jug. Add nutmeg, and salt and pepper. Whisk with a fork to combine.
- Arrange a layer of potatoes over base of prepared dish. Top with a layer of onion. Drizzle with a little cream mixture. Repeat layers until all ingredients have been used.

- Cover dish tightly with foil. Bake for 30 to 40 minutes or until potatoes are just tender. Remove foil. Cook for a further 30 minutes or until top is golden.

Nutrition Information

- Calories: 481.585 calories
- Total Fat: 32.5 grams fat
- Saturated Fat: 20.1 grams saturated fat
- Total Carbohydrate: 44 grams carbohydrates
- Sugar: 4.1 grams sugar
- Protein: 6.1 grams protein
- Sodium: 74 milligrams sodium
- Cholesterol: 115 milligrams cholesterol

68. Simple Potato Bake

Serving: 6 | Prep: 10mins | Ready in: 100mins

Ingredients

- 2/3 cup (165ml) milk
- 2/3 cup (165ml) thickened cream
- 1/2 teaspoon freshly grated nutmeg
- 2 garlic cloves, finely chopped
- 600g sebago potatoes, peeled, thinly sliced (a mandoline is ideal)
- 50g unsalted butter, chopped

Direction

- Preheat oven to 180°C. Grease a 1.5L baking dish. Combine milk, cream, nutmeg and garlic in a bowl, then season.
- Place a single layer of potato in the dish, then pour over a little milk mixture. Continue layers, finishing with a layer of potato. Dot the top with butter.
- Cover dish with baking paper, then foil. Bake for 1 hour. Uncover and bake for a further 25-30 minutes until golden and tender. Stand for 10 minutes, then serve.

Nutrition Information

- Calories: 191.917 calories
- Total Fat: 12.1 grams fat
- Total Carbohydrate: 18.4 grams carbohydrates
- Sugar: 2.5 grams sugar
- Saturated Fat: 7.6 grams saturated fat
- Protein: 3.4 grams protein
- Cholesterol: 30 milligrams cholesterol
- Sodium: 79 milligrams sodium

69. Slow Cooked Sweet Potato Bake

Serving: 6 | Prep: 20mins | Ready in: 110mins

Ingredients

- 50g butter, chopped
- 2 red onions, thinly sliced
- 2 teaspoons finely chopped thyme leaves
- 2 garlic cloves, crushed
- pinch ground nutmeg
- 1kg sweet potato, peeled, very thinly sliced (see notes)
- 80g gruyere, finely grated
- 1 cup Massel vegetable liquid stock
- 1 cup grated mozzarella

Direction

- Preheat oven to 200C or 180C fan-forced. Grease a 5 cup ovenproof baking dish.
- Melt butter in a large frying pan over medium-high heat. Cook onion and thyme, stirring, for 5 minutes. Reduce heat to medium and cook, stirring, for 5 minutes or until softened (but not coloured). Stir through garlic and nutmeg and cook for 1 minute or until fragrant. Season.
- Arrange sweet potato in prepared dish, in flat layers, interspersing with onion mixture and half of gruyere. Press down. Pour over Massel Liquid Stock Vegetable Style. Cover with foil and bake for 1 hour. Remove foil, top with combined mozzarella and remaining gruyere and bake for another 15 minutes or until golden and tender.
- Serve with salad, if desired.

70. Swede, Potato And Bacon Gratin

Serving: 6 | Prep: 15mins | Ready in: 95mins

Ingredients

- 4 bacon rashers, coarsely chopped
- 1 large swede, peeled, thinly sliced
- 4 large potatoes, thinly sliced
- 1 brown onion, thinly sliced
- 1 garlic clove, thinly sliced
- 6 thyme sprigs
- 2 teaspoons coarsely chopped rosemary
- 300ml thickened cream
- 1/2 cup (125ml) chicken stock
- 1/2 cup (60g) coarsely grated tasty cheddar
- Thyme sprigs, extra, to serve

Direction

- Preheat oven to 180C. Grease a 6-cup (1.5L) ovenproof dish.
- Cook the bacon in a medium frying pan over medium heat, stirring occasionally, for 5 mins or until golden brown.
- Layer the swede, potato, onion, garlic, thyme, rosemary and bacon in the prepared dish. Combine cream and stock in a small bowl. Season. Pour evenly over the potato mixture.
- Bake for 50 mins-1 hour or until potato and swede are tender and gratin is golden brown. Sprinkle with cheddar. Bake for 15 mins or until golden brown. Set aside for 5 mins to cool slightly.

Nutrition Information

- Calories: 393.633 calories
- Sugar: 6 grams sugar

- Protein: 14 grams protein
- Total Fat: 23 grams fat
- Saturated Fat: 14 grams saturated fat
- Sodium: 720 milligrams sodium
- Total Carbohydrate: 30 grams carbohydrates

71. Sweet Potato And Ricotta Bake

Serving: 4 | Prep: 15mins | Ready in: 85mins

Ingredients

- 1kg red sweet potatoes, very thinly sliced
- 500g gold sweet potatoes, very thinly sliced
- 1 spring onion, thinly sliced
- 150g fresh ricotta, crumbled
- 1 rosemary sprig, torn
- 1 garlic clove, thinly sliced
- 1/4 cup (20g) finely grated parmesan
- 40g butter, melted
- Rosemary sprigs, torn, to serve

Direction

- Preheat oven 180C. Grease a 24cm round baking dish.
- Arrange the sweet potato slices upright in the prepared dish. Sprinkle with the onion, ricotta, rosemary, garlic and parmesan. Drizzle with the butter.
- Cover with a piece of greased foil and cook for 50 mins. Uncover and cook for a further 20 mins or until sweet potato is tender and golden brown. Sprinkle with extra rosemary to serve.

72. Sweet Potato Bake

Serving: 8 | Prep: 30mins | Ready in: 80mins

Ingredients

- 550g white or purple sweet potato, scrubbed or peeled, thinly sliced
- 700g orange sweet potato, scrubbed or peeled, thinly sliced
- 2 teaspoons olive oil
- 1 leek, trimmed, thinly sliced
- 150g crème fraîche
- 150ml milk
- 1 garlic clove, crushed
- 1 tablespoon chopped fresh sage
- 55g parmesan, finely grated
- 50g vintage cheddar, coarsely grated
- Fresh baby herbs, to serve (optional)

Direction

- Preheat oven to 200C/180C fan forced. Lightly grease a 6.5cm-deep, 20 x 30cm baking dish.
- Place the sweet potato in a large microwave-safe bowl with 60ml (1/4 cup) water. Cover with 2 sheets of plastic wrap. Cook in the microwave on High for 8 minutes or until just tender. Remove and drain. (Alternatively, you can steam the sweet potato.)
- Meanwhile, heat the oil in a small non-stick frying pan over medium heat. Add the leek and cook, stirring, for 3-4 minutes or until the leek is softened and lightly golden. Remove from heat.
- Whisk together the crème fraiche, milk, garlic and sage in a jug. Season.
- Layer the sweet potato, leek and parmesan in the prepared dish until all the ingredients have been used. Sprinkle with the cheddar. Pour the milk mixture evenly over the top. Season with pepper.
- Bake for 35-40 minutes or until the top is golden and cheese has melted. Set aside for 10 minutes before serving. Sprinkle with baby herbs, if you like.

Nutrition Information

- Calories: 272.938 calories
- Total Fat: 13 grams fat
- Saturated Fat: 8 grams saturated fat

- Total Carbohydrate: 28 grams carbohydrates
- Protein: 8 grams protein

73. Sweet Potato Bake With Bacon Crumble

Serving: 0 | Prep: 30mins | Ready in: 120mins

Ingredients

- 850g orange sweet potato, peeled
- 1 cup milk or cream
- 40g butter
- 1 small onion, finely sliced into rings
- 2 bay leaves
- 200g Primo Rindless Short Cut Bacon, chopped
- 70g (1 cup) fresh wholegrain breadcrumbs
- 1 clove garlic, crushed
- 25g butter, melted
- 2 tablespoons maple syrup
- 40g (1/2 cup) grated tasty cheese
- 1/4 bunch fresh sage

Direction

- Preheat oven to 190C/170C fan-forced. Cut sweet potato into 2mm slices. Combine milk or cream, butter and bay leaves in a heatproof jug. Cover with plastic wrap. Place in the microwave oven, on High for 1 minute. Leave to infuse for 5 minutes.
- Lay sweet potato slices in overlapping layers in a 21cm round, 8cm deep ovenproof dish. Scatter over a third of the onion slices. Repeat with two more layers, finishing with a final sweet potato layer. Pour the infused milk or cream mixture over the sweet potato. Cover with a sheet of non-stick baking paper and foil. Bake for 1 hour or until potato slices are tender.
- Meanwhile, to make crumble, heat a non-stick frying pan over medium heat. Add bacon and cook, stirring for 4-5 minutes or until almost crisp. Remove from heat. Place breadcrumbs in a large bowl, then add bacon, garlic, butter and syrup. Mix well. Stir in cheese and sage and season with salt and pepper.
- Remove foil and baking paper from baked sweet potato and discard bay leaves. Scatter with the crumble mixture. Bake uncovered for a further 15 minutes or until golden and crisp on top. Leave for 10 minutes before serving.

74. Sweet Potato With Pecan Ginger Crumble

Serving: 8 | Prep: 0S | Ready in:

Ingredients

- 1kg orange sweet potato, peeled, thinly sliced
- 1/2 medium red onion, thinly sliced
- 1 cup Massel chicken style liquid stock
- 1 tablespoon wholegrain mustard
- 80g butter, chopped
- 1/4 cup brown sugar
- 1/2 cup plain flour
- 1/2 teaspoon ground ginger
- 1/2 cup pecans, roughly chopped (see note)
- Chopped fresh flat-leaf parsley leaves, to serve

Direction

- Preheat oven to 220°C/ 200°C fan-forced. Layer potato and onion in an 8 cup-capacity ovenproof dish. Combine stock and mustard in a jug. Pour over sweet potato. Cover tightly with foil. Bake for 30 minutes or until potato is just tender.
- Meanwhile, rub butter, sugar, flour and ginger together in a bowl until combined. Add pecans. Rub to combine.
- Remove foil from dish. Sprinkle butter mixture over sweet potato. Bake for 10 minutes or until golden. Serve.

Nutrition Information

- Calories: 268.636 calories
- Saturated Fat: 6 grams saturated fat
- Total Carbohydrate: 30 grams carbohydrates
- Total Fat: 14 grams fat
- Sugar: 13 grams sugar
- Protein: 4 grams protein
- Sodium: 241.99 milligrams sodium

Nutrition Information

- Calories: 790.851 calories
- Total Carbohydrate: 34 grams carbohydrates
- Protein: 27 grams protein
- Cholesterol: 175 milligrams cholesterol
- Sodium: 1291.22 milligrams sodium
- Total Fat: 59 grams fat
- Saturated Fat: 35 grams saturated fat
- Sugar: 5 grams sugar

75. Tartiflette (cheese Potato Bake)

Serving: 4 | Prep: 10mins | Ready in: 70mins

Ingredients

- 1kg pontiac potatoes, peeled, roughly chopped
- 50g unsalted butter
- 1 onion, chopped
- 2 garlic cloves, finely chopped
- 2 teaspoons chopped thyme leaves
- 200g piece speck* or pancetta, cut into 1cm cubes
- 1/2 cup (125ml) dry white wine
- 200ml thickened cream
- 250g reblochon* or raclette* cheese, grated

Direction

- Preheat the oven to 200°C.
- Place the potato in a large pan of cold salted water. Bring to the boil over high heat and cook for 3 minutes. Drain well.
- Melt the butter in a large fry pan over medium-low heat. Add the onion and cook, stirring occasionally, for 5 minutes or until soft. Add the garlic, thyme and speck or pancetta, and cook, stirring, for 5 minutes. Stir in the wine, cream, potato and most of the cheese.
- Transfer the mixture to a large baking dish and top with remaining cheese. Cover with baking paper to prevent the cheese sticking, then a layer of foil. Bake for 20 minutes, then remove the foil and baking paper. Bake for a further 20 minutes or until bubbling and golden.

Index

B
Bacon 3,7,9,15,27,35,40,42
Basil 16
Beef 3,28,31
Bran 1,2
Brie 3,7
Butter 34

C
Cake 3,25
Celeriac 3,7,11,32
Cheese 3,18,19,20,35,36
Chicken 3,37,38
Cream 3,11,12,13,14,15,16,19,24,26,28,38
Crumble 3,29,42

D
Dijon mustard 10

F
Fat 3,5,7,8,9,10,11,12,13,14,15,16,17,18,19,20,21,22,24,25,26,27,28,29,30,31,32,33,34,35,36,37,38,39,40,41,43
Fennel 3,20,33
Fresh coriander 12,28

G
Garlic 3,17,19,21,37
Gin 3,42
Gnocchi 3,24
Gratin 3,5,14,20,22,24,26,29,30,31,33,34,35,40

H
Ham 3,13,22

K
Kale 3,12,14

L
Lamb 3,5
Lasagne 3,31
Leek 3,22,29,33,35,38
Lemon 28

M
Mustard 3,28

N
Nut 3,5,7,8,9,10,11,12,13,14,15,17,18,19,20,21,22,24,25,26,27,28,29,30,31,32,33,34,35,36,37,39,40,41,42,43

O
Olive 12,13,27,38
Onion 3,30

P
Pancetta 3,10
Parmesan 3,26,29
Parsnip 3,29,31
Pasta 19,31
Pecan 3,5,29,42
Peel 11,21
Pesto 3,16
Pie 3,20
Potato 1,3,4,5,6,7,8,9,10,11,12,13,14,15,16,17,18,19,20,21,22,23,24,25,26,27,28,29,30,31,32,33,34,35,36,37,38,39,40,41,42,43
Prosciutto 3,36
Pumpkin 3,11,12,24

R

Ricotta 3,41

Rocket 3,16

Rosemary 3,13,15,21,37,41

S

Salad 5

Salt 25,29,34,35

Scallop 3,16,21,39

Stock 40

Sugar 7,8,10,13,15,16,21,22,25,26,29,30,35,36,37,39,40,43

Swede 3,40

T

Tea 10,18

Thyme 3,7,17,21,40

Tomato 3,19

W

White pepper 9

Conclusion

Thank you again for downloading this book!

I hope you enjoyed reading about my book!

If you enjoyed this book, please take the time to share your thoughts and post a review on Amazon. It'd be greatly appreciated!

Write me an honest review about the book – I truly value your opinion and thoughts and I will incorporate them into my next book, which is already underway.

Thank you!

If you have any questions, **feel free to contact at:** *author@roastroastroast.com*

Joy Brannon

roastroastroast.com

Printed in the USA
CPSIA information can be obtained
at www.ICGtesting.com
LVHW081038311024
795306LV00063B/958